Front: Portrait of George McCorquodale (1817-1895).
It was originally in the main offices in King Street,
London and is now in the hands of the family.

Opposite:

Top Left: McCorquodale family crest.

Top Right: Kate McCorquodale (1822-1870).

Bottom Left: London & North Western Railway Logo.

Bottom Right: McCorquodale letter heading.

A Printer's Dream.

One day, some time ago, in the early years of the Victorian age a Liverpool to Manchester
train pulled slowly and noisily into Newton Bridge Station. Among the numerous people
alighting from the carriages was a sturdy looking man sporting a thick, luxuriant beard.
He possessed a brisk, efficient manner as he leapt down from the train and gazed about him.
On his left was a very busy station building but on his right loomed a large impressive
structure known as the Legh Arms Hotel. Initially he paused, glancing at the hotel,
before striding quickly down a cobbled road that ran between them to the village of Newton.
Passing the two buildings he arrived before a large, strange construction on his right,
more in the shape of a Greek Temple, seemingly out of place in that rural setting.
The man stopped, he seemed to be lost in thought for a few moments and he then
nodded as if he was making a major decision. The year was 1846 and
George McCorquodale, printer and stationer of Liverpool, had arrived in
Newton and the printing world would never be the same again.

George McCorquodale

Master Printer

Foreword

My Great Grandfather, George McCorquodale, was one of those entrepreneurs
of Scottish origin who started businesses in Lancashire in the 19th century.
His printing business grew from very small beginnings in Liverpool to become a
worldwide company. Much of his early work was for the new railways and
famous local names such as Pilkington and Beecham.
Geoff Simm has discovered his ancestors from the mists of ancient times and has
explored his business career and those of his sons and grandsons through
arduous and expert research to produce a book which will be of interest to many.

Colin McCorquodale.

Also By Geoff Simm:-

Richard Evans of Haydock.

Mining Memories – with Ian Winstanley.

In Affectionate Remembrance – with Ian Winstanley.

Parkside Colliery.

The Life and Times of Peter Legh the Younger.

A Picture of Newton-le-Willows.

The Leghs and Haydock Coal.

Acknowledgements

Having just retired I was spending some time studying the Victorian census returns for Newton-le-Willows. During this project I became intrigued with the number of people employed by McCorquodales, the local printing firm. Nearly every household in the Newton area, comprising High Street, Mercer Street, Birley Street, Mill Lane and even further afield had family members employed by the firm. It then occurred to me what a great influence this company had had on our local town and how little was on public display to that effect. So began my quest into the life of the founder of the company - George McCorquodale. It was a journey that took me to all parts of the country visiting people and places connected to the company.

Initially my research began locally getting in contact with people I knew were connected to the firm. My first breakthrough was information provided by John Kilshaw, a friend of mine for over fifty years. He had worked for McCorquodales and produced the phone numbers of two of the managers: Roy Carter and Peter Aspinall. They were able to give me information and an insight into the politics and working practices of the   company. Roy and Peter also produced other contacts such as John Bambery, Eric   Eustance and Geoff Dee. Also about the same time Pat Harrop contacted me and kindly handed over the research she had done for the local history group about the company. Then came a stroke of luck that sometimes can occur during local history research. I had decided to contact by letter as many McCorquodales as I could find. I only sent one letter. The man I sent the letter to, Colin Norman McCorquodale, replied immediately. He was the family's historian and was able to provide everything I needed about the history, ancient and modern, of the McCorquodale family. Colin introduced me to other members of the McCorquodale family such as John Lockart Wood, Hamish Norman McCorquodale and Sally McCorquodale who with their enthusiasm and assistance have helped me greatly.

Besides contacting people I began pursuing the early records of George McCorquodale and the beginnings of the company in the Central Library of Liverpool and the St. Helens Local History & Archives Library. I would like to give a special thanks to the ladies of the Liverpool Family History Society who in ten minutes solved a problem that had dogged me for six months. Other people who have assisted me and I truly thank are Kate M. Atkinson, David Pill, Steven Dowd, Neil Forshaw, Andrew Fackey, Richard Thomas and my ever suffering wife Susan. If I have forgotten anybody I apologise.

But my greatest thanks must go to Colin Norman McCorquodale. He has assisted me every step of the way and has made this book possible.

The journey into the life of George McCorquodale has taken me nearly three years and it has been full of surprises, delights and shocks - but it has been worth it! It is now time to put George McCorquodale and the firm of McCorquodale & Co. back on the local map. This book makes an attempt to do that.

One confession I have to make is that I have never been involved in the printing industry. I've never been a Printer, Compositor, Reader, Binder, Sewer, Ruler or even a 'Clicker' and I've never been on a Waysgooze - but I probably would have enjoyed it greatly.

Geoff Simm.

Introduction

Looking back in the industrial history of our country it becomes evident that powerful families were the driving force behind the far reaching changes which were occurring in the country. They were dynamic, autocratic, innovative, ruthless, controlling but most of the time were benevolent and paternalistic. In some cases they made an industry their own, probably destroying all other opposition. In recent years the important part that they played in the industrial revolution has been criticised or played down. But without their drive, enthusiasm and pride the country would have been a different place today. Entrepreneurial families and individuals became synonymous with certain industries producing many diverse products. Recognisable names easily spring to mind such as the Pilkingtons in the glass industry, Stephensons in railways and locomotives, Cadbury in chocolate, Colman in mustard and many, many others. One prime example of the industrial entrepreneurs was Josiah Wedgwood. He wasn't just a potter but a complete business man and an influential reformer as well. He was a man who was industrially aware, had an ability to make money, was in the forefront of labour relations, understood marketing, technology, education and possessed a strong sense of morality. The entrepreneurs of Britain, good, bad or indifferent, were a vital part in the development and history of the country.

In the ever competitive printing industry, although it may be disputed in some quarters, it will always be the name of McCorquodale that springs to mind – a company that rose from humble beginnings to become an international power. Initially they were closely linked to the great railway expansion of the Victorian age and were always referred to as the railway printers. But later the company expanded into all forms of printing and even took on much of the printing work for the government. The founder of the firm was George McCorquodale (1817-1895) and he possessed all the attributes referred to above of a typical industrial entrepreneur. He was shrewd, ambitious, clear-headed and a driven man. Through him McCorquodale & Co. became one of the largest and most respected printing companies in the country.

George McCorquodale

(1817 - 1895)

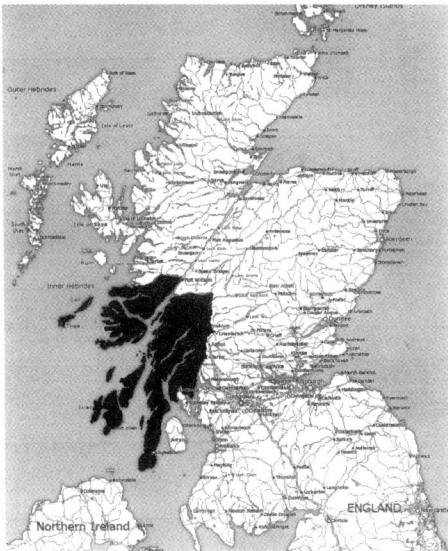

Argyllshire

McOrcadale — McCorqtadel?
I duly having stopped to spell
The variations which appear
In correspondence through the year,
Considered its origination,
And proceeded with investigation.
It seems that whilst the Pict and Scot,
Were sorting out their common lot,
Up in a Scandinavian Fjord,
Lived a certain Viking war lord,
A Norseman – name of Thorketill,
The keeper of the war god's kettle.
On sailing with a longship raid,
Intending Scotland to invade,
He ran into a gale which blew his
Boat up on the Butt of Lewis.
Thorketill stayed – it came to pass
Enamoured by a local lass,
And up by Stornoway there dwelt
Invading Norse and Native Celt.
Succeeding generation passed,
The Thorketills were Scots at last,
Thus custom stated that each male
Henceforth be called – MacC'orcadail.
The son of Olaf, King of Man,
Leod of the Lewis, formed a clan,
And hearing it was highly rated,
Macs sept became affiliated.
So ere James on Flodden Field lay dead,
Or Edward fro' Bannockburn had fled,
Before the loch-bound mystery,
McCORQUODALE was history.

Inveraray

Family Roots

The Scottish Clan of McCorquodale originated in the Argyllshire area. The surname McCorquodale came from the Anglicisation of the Gaelic Mac Thocadail which meant son of Torcadal. The name Torcadal was of Norse origin and referred to Thor's kettle or a cauldron of the thunder spirit. The name conjures up stories from the Scandinavian legends of long ago when raiders plundered the coastline of the British Isles and then finally settled. Even in the family there are stories of pacts made and broken between tribal lords and the struggle for land. The McCorquodales lay claim to a lineage that stretched back to a certain Thorkil who, because he rescued the head of Kenneth Mac Alpin's father, was awarded lands in the Argyllshire area. Kenneth Mac Alpin, a legendary figure in Scots history, was at the time King of the Scots. The Scots were centred in the Argyllshire area and were involved in a fierce struggle with the Picts, who controlled the rest of the country. A more definite history was referred to in the 15th century when the Barons McCorquodale held lands west of Loch Awe. They were based at Phantelane – the white island of Loch Tromlee – where their castle was located. The ruins of the castle still survive today where the barons once ruled. The McCorquodales were well established by the 17th century when Duncan McCorquodale was appointed Justice of the Peace by none other than Oliver Cromwell. However in the same century some members of the family had become associated with the MacGregors and were known to be notorious thieves.

In the 18th century the last of the Baron McCorquodales died and that left the clan without a chief, a situation that has carried on until the present day. The McCorquodales, like many of the Scottish clans, are very passionate about their heritage and are rightfully proud of their crest and tartan. Although their clan is not as famous as the Macgregors, Camerons and such like, they are still a distinct clan in their own right. The modern Clan McCorquodale although recognised by the Lord Lyon King of Arms has no legal standing under Scots Law because it has no recognised chief. However its members are permitted to wear a crest badge which shows their allegiance to the clan.

On page 10 is a piece of prose penned in the 1960s regarding the different spellings of the family name and its lineage. It was often used in the company's magazines relating to the problems that employees had with the spelling in a world-wide market and the different connotations that appeared in their correspondence. The poem itself was written by Olive Wilkinson a lady of some note in the Cashier's department at the Newton works. Olive came from Ashton-in-Makerfield; she never married but was known for her literary compositions and was a leading member of the local Girl Guides.

The line of the family from which George McCorquodale descended was based near Inveraray, a small town on the shores of Loch Fyne. It was at that time a port and also the ancestral home of the Dukes of Argyll. At various times in the family's history members had been appointed to the post of Sheriff Officer in Inveraray. In Scotland Sheriffs were officers of the courts who served documents and enforced court orders. At one time the McCorquodale family owned a trading ship as well as running the local hostelry. The shipping trade in the area was probably of the coastal form but could have stretched as far afield as Ireland and France. Loch Fyne was a long slender sea-loch with good access to the open sea suitable for that type of trade. Hugh McCorquodale, the father of George McCorquodale, was born in Inveraray in 1764. He was the sixth child of Archibald and Anne McCorquodale, the family consisting of 5 sons and 4 daughters.

His eldest brother Alexander became Sheriff of Inveraray, carrying on a family tradition that stretched back a number of generations. Hugh and his other brothers probably earned their living out of the merchant trade previously mentioned. At one time their fortunes took a bit of a down turn when their ship was wrecked. However the problem was that they were smuggling French brandy and being pursued by government customs officers along Loch Fyne! Whether the brush with the law resulted in the rapid departure of Hugh to pastures new it is not known but is a possibility. At one time the financial downturn in the family's circumstances resulted in a large number of them emigrating to all parts of the world even as far as Argentina. There is rumour, from family sources, that Hugh lived and worked in Glasgow or Edinburgh for a number of years but this has not been proved. Nonetheless at the end of the 18th century Hugh McCorquodale aged 35 left the country of his birth to seek fame and fortune in the rapidly expanding city of Liverpool in Lancashire. At the end of the eighteenth century the port of Liverpool had been developing for nearly one hundred years. The first enclosed dock in the modern world was constructed there as far back as 1715. Due to its success further docks were produced and by the end of eighteenth century Liverpool had become one of the great ports in the world, controlling over 40% of the world's trade. The population of the port during that time grew from 6,000 to 80,000 due to the great success of the shipping enterprise. Because of its position on the western coast of Britain it also became one of the key ports in the slave trade and that further advanced the wealth of the port. Liverpool must have been a massive attraction to Hugh McCorquodale and it proved to be perfect for his purposes. He was hard working, ambitious and wanted to become wealthy. Hugh was conversant with shipping and had been a merchant for a number of years therefore Liverpool, at the beginning of the 19th century, was the ideal location for his new career. Hugh McCorquodale first appeared in Liverpool in 1800 listed as a merchant with offices in Pownall Street and Liver Street, two streets only a short distance from the river frontage and the ever busy docks. A few years after his arrival in Liverpool Hugh married in 1803 Lucia Hall, the daughter of George Hall. He was 39 and his bride was 20.

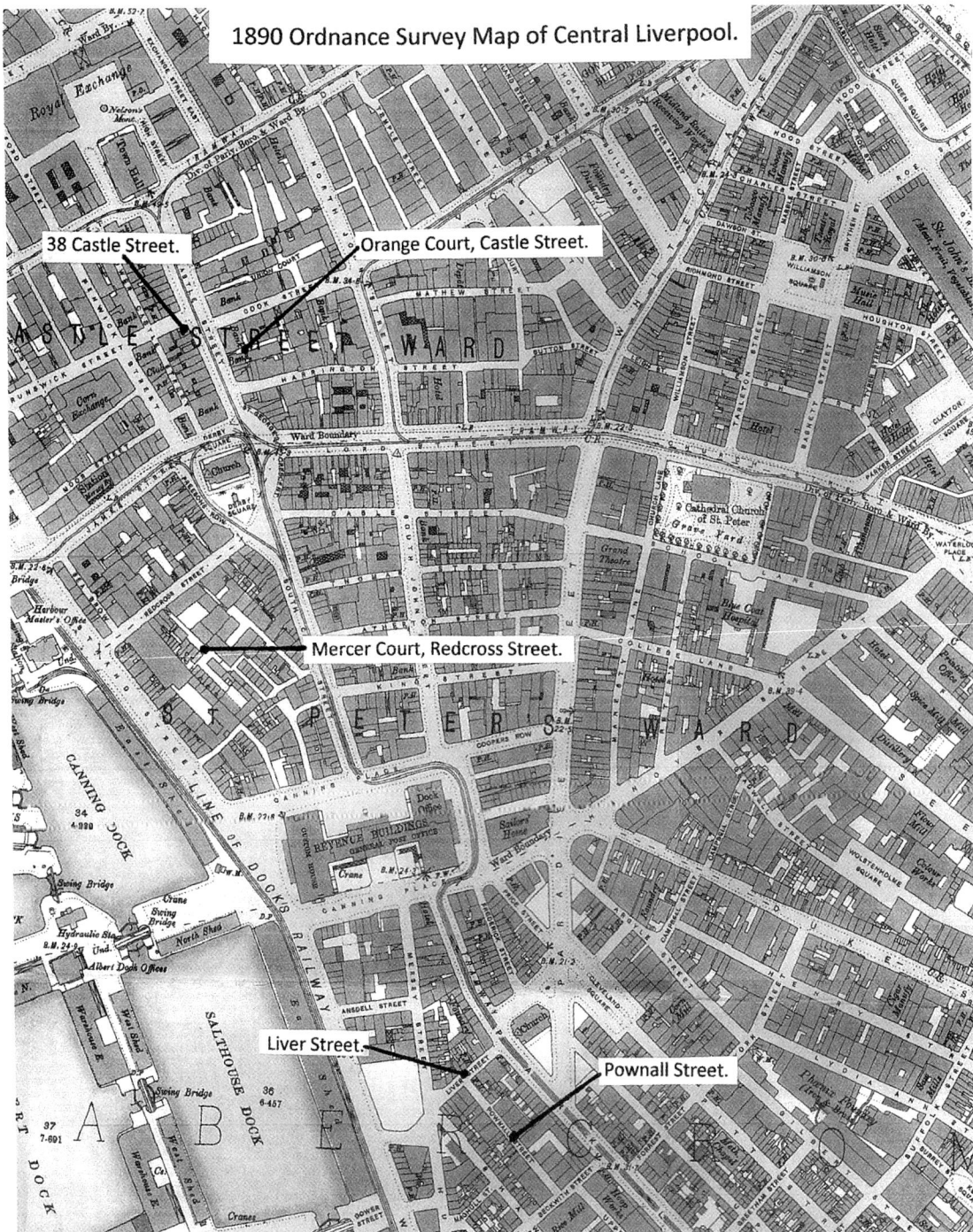

1890 Ordnance Survey Map of Central Liverpool.

38 Castle Street.

Orange Court, Castle Street.

Mercer Court, Redcross Street.

Liver Street.

Pownall Street.

A composite map showing the various places in Liverpool centre connected with Hugh and George McCorquodale.

He probably travelled back to Scotland for his marriage because his wife's family was based in Edinburgh. His father-in-law was reported to be a merchant both in Dundee and London. Over the next 18 years Hugh and Lucia had 8 children, Helen, Lucia, Hugh, John Hall, Anne, Alexander, George and Elizabeth Mary. After his move to Liverpool and subsequent marriage to Lucia Hall, Hugh McCorquodale began attending local Church of England churches but soon reverted back to his old Presbyterianism. Before 1793 there was no place of worship for the many Presbyterians who had moved from Scotland to Liverpool. A small group of Presbyterians led by a Dr. John McCulloch raised enough money to build a Kirk on Oldham Street, Liverpool. It was opened in 1793 with seating for over 800 people and that was the church that Hugh and his family used whilst he was in the city. Hugh & Lucia McCorquodale selected a rather unusual method of baptising their children. Firstly they used the local Church of England churches and in some cases had the child christened again at the Oldham Street Kirk. However in the case of three of the boys they had them baptised at Churches in Scotland but had the event recorded in the Oldham Street Kirk. Hugh jr. was baptised by the Rev. Dr. James Nairne of Pittenweem, Fife, Alexander was baptised by the Rev. Dr. Pebie of Linlithgow and George was baptised by the Rev. Dr. Chalmers of Glasgow.

Thomas Chalmers (1780-1847) was the minister of St. George's Tron Parish Church, Glasgow. He became one of the most influential leaders of the Church of Scotland and the Free Church of Scotland and has been called Scotland's greatest nineteenth century churchman. It must be said that George McCorquodale was destined for greatness to be baptised by such a man.

Hugh McCorquodale's house
Rodney Street, Liverpool

Initially on the career front Hugh probably found it difficult to establish himself as a merchant being new to the area. However within twelve months at the beginning of 1801 he combined with two other merchants to form the company McIver, McViccar & McCorquodale. It proved to be a shrewd move because the McIver family was involved in all aspects of ship equipment and the McViccar family had been established as merchants in Liverpool for over 15 years. The connection of Hugh McCorquodale to the company was confirmed by the present day family who still tell the story of McIver, McViccar and McCorquodale saying that they were not well liked and were known to their competitors as McAdder, McViper and McCrocodile. Family stories usually have a grain of truth at the bottom of them and that has proved correct with this McCorquodale tale.

Throughout his time as a merchant in Liverpool Hugh McCorquodale never moved his business address from Pownall Street, staying there for over 20 years. Hugh's first home in Liverpool was in Great Charlotte Street but he soon moved to Wolstenholme Square and then Rodney Street in 1807. At that time Rodney Street was just being developed and his house was one of the earliest built. Rodney Street has always been associated with the medical profession and it has retained many of its original buildings to the present day. Hugh stayed there for the next 5 years and then moved to Grove Cottage, Toxteth Park. This was to be the family home for the next 20 years. The area known as Toxteth was originally a royal park so there had been no development during that time. In the 17th century Toxteth land was made available to farmers and industrialists. That resulted, over the next hundred years, in large numbers of industrial buildings and residences being built, some of a grand appearance some not so grand. During the 19th century it became home to the large mansions built by the prosperous Liverpool merchants. Hugh and Lucia McCorquodale, plus their quickly increasing family, were able to settle at Grove Cottage for a number of years. Very little has survived detailing the Merchant career of Hugh McCorquodale even in the family archives. However the activities of the company appear in the Billinge's Liverpool Advertiser and Marine Intelligencer. It was a weekly newspaper that gave information on the movement of ships, their destinations and the goods that were being sold in the city. McIver, McViccar & McCorquodale were using a number of ships to various destinations such as Madeira, New York, Jamaica, Nova Scotia and Georgia. Most of the imported products were sold either at the dock or at Joseph McViccar's premises on Castle Street. The company sold on such articles as Mahogany, Barrel Staves, Tobacco, Georgia Cotton and American Flour. Activity at the port was at its peak during the summer months and in 1802 they were using three ships, the Montezuma, Rufus and Elizabeth, carrying cargo and passengers to Charleston, Savannah and Wilmington respectively.

Other merchant companies active at that time were Rathbone, Hughes & Duncan, Humble, Holland & Hurry and John & Robert Gladstone. But of course Liverpool was known for its infamous role in the slave trade. The port was the focal point in the triangular trade that connected Britain with West Africa and the Americas. The involvement of the company of McIver, McViccar and McCorquodale can be proved because of a surviving document of 1804 which begins:-

"Account Sales of 197 Negroes received by Brig Mars on account of Messrs McIver, McViccar & McCorquodale Merchants Liverpool."

This is the title of a five page report and takes the form of a series of ingoings and outgoings regarding the sale of slaves in Savannah, Georgia in the Americas. It was compiled by Benjamin Maurice who was the agent for the three merchants and checked by Joseph Arnold who was the local Auctioneer. The people who purchased the slaves are shown, the prices, what the slaves ate, medicines used on them, the clothes that were purchased for them, the captain's wages, the pilot's charges and other outgoings related to the trade. All monies are shown in dollars except the salary of Captain White who insisted in being paid in pounds. The price for a male slave was in the region of 400 dollars but a rebate would be given if a number was bought. Women were sold for about 325 dollars and children 300 dollars. They were fed on slops which probably came from local food outlets. Over the two month extent of the document five of the slaves were reported to have died in their holding pen.

In 1807 due to the concern over the impending abolition of the slave trade, the Gore's directory of Liverpool listed all of the merchants involved in the trade. The list showed no member of the company so they must have ceased their connection by that time. The slave trade act was passed in the British Parliament on 25th March 1807. It abolished the slave trade in the British Empire but not slavery itself. That had to wait for 26 years before its abolition. Great Britain was one of the first countries in the world to abolish the slave trade. The merchant firm of McIver, McViccar and McCorquodale lasted until 1810 when the company was dissolved and the three men went their different ways.

For CHARLESTON,
(Daily expected to arrive)
The American Ship MONTEZUMA,
THOMAS MORGAN, Master.
A well known fast failing vessel. The greater part of her cargo being already engaged, she will return without delay. For freight, &c. apply to
McIVER, McVICCAR and McCORQUODALE.

For SAVANNAH, in GEORGIA,
The American Ship R U F U S,
JOHN HOLLAND, Master,
Burthen about 250 tons, a remarkable fast failing vessel; the greater part of her cargo being engaged, is intended to fail by the 12th July.——For freight or passage apply to Capt Holland on board in Queen's Dock, or to
McIVER, McVICCAR and McCORQUODALE.

For WILMINGTON, NORTH CAROLINA,
The American Brigt. ELIZABETH,
WM. AIKIN, Master.
Burthen about 250 tons; the principal part of her cargo being ready to put on board, is intended to fail in a few days. For freight or passage apply to
McIVER, McVICCAR, McCORQUODALE.

Shipping information – Billinge's Liverpool Advertiser - 1802

Family sources say that the company was not successful and went bankrupt but they did last for nearly 10 years and it could have been that Hugh, after gaining experience as a Liverpool merchant, decided to branch out on his own.

After 1810 Hugh McCorquodale carried on as an individual merchant for a further 12 years, sometimes successfully, sometimes suffering failures. It was a trying time for the Liverpool merchants. The Napoleonic war was raging and most of Europe was in turmoil. Also the abolition of the lucrative slave trade must have had an effect on the port. Another trading problem appeared in 1812 with the commencement of the war between Britain and America. It lasted for over two years. Most of the north of America was blockaded by the Royal Navy and any form of shipping was drastically reduced.

Then in 1823 there was a complete change in his career when Hugh purchased a Tailor and Drapery business at 14 Bold Street, Liverpool. It was on part of the site now occupied by Waterstone's large bookshop but probably in an earlier building. Over the next twelve years Hugh amassed enough of a fortune to retire and enjoy some leisure time with his family. He was well over 70 and his wife was in her mid-fifties when the decision was made in 1837 to move back to Edinburgh, her home town. At first they lived at 1 Gayfield Place, an impressive Georgian building, of four storeys, just a short walk from Princes Street and the city centre. Later they moved to 10 St John Street in the centre of the old city. In the 1841 Scottish census the family is listed at that address with George McCorquodale being described as a clerk.

Moray House, Edinburgh

Hugh McCorquodale's last residence in Edinburgh was Moray House, a fine 17th century building now part of the university. His wife died in 1844 and that may have prompted him to return to Liverpool. He lived at Laurel Cottage on Smithdown Lane in Liverpool for the rest of his days. When he died there in 1848 his son Alexander, who at that time was living in Russell Street, was in attendance. Laurel Cottage was lived in by a number of the McCorquodales over the next few years. Two sons, Hugh and George, as well as his daughter Helen made their homes there.

The Arrival Of George

George McCorquodale was born at Grove Cottage, Toxteth Park, Liverpool on the 10th of May 1817. The building and its environs was described in the 1890s in the following way:-

"The White House. This was a farm house and is shown in the fields marked 'Parrs' on Perry's Map in 1768. As late as 1850 a well kept garden containing many trees, flourished on its north side and it is hardly two years since the old well, which was on the south side near the present pavement in Mill Street, covered with an old mill stone, was filled up. This, at one time, was its only source of water supply. The name 'Grove Cottage,' – reminiscent of the whispering trees – still remains over the doorway nearest the road."

George grew up in a stable, settled family that had not moved from the same house for a number of years. By all accounts he was always close to his brothers and sisters, not losing contact with them throughout their lifetimes. In the future his two surviving brothers became merchants in their own right following the early career of their father. The eldest son, Hugh jr. was an importer and merchant based in Liverpool. He was married in New York to Helen Pitcain, the daughter of the American Consul at Hamburg.

"GROVE COTTAGE,"

The other brother, Alexander, worked in the same building as George carrying on the business of a commission agent for an insurance company before moving to Glasgow. He later became a successful merchant in Leith and also had connections with San Francisco. After the 1860s Alexander lived in Portobello, which later became a Victorian beach resort. It was a few miles east of Edinburgh centre, between Holyrood Park and the sea. Three of George's sisters, all of them unmarried, followed him to Newton and lived nearby at various times during the 19th century. Two of them, Lucia and Helen, are buried there but Elizabeth spent the last of her days in Edinburgh, dying at Hamilton Lodge in 1888.

George grew up in Liverpool and family sources state that his father put him into a good Liverpool school. However due to one of the downturns in his father's finances, he was taken out of school and sent to work at a local firm. The significance was that it was a printing company and George McCorquodale, the future head of countrywide company, became a printer's devil. A printer's devil was an apprentice who performed most of the dirty tasks such as mixing inks and carrying type. It is said that they were called devils because they were always black from the ink! Historically George was not on his own, because such people as Benjamin Franklin, Thomas Jefferson and Walt Whitman also carried out that sort of work.

George moved to Edinburgh with his father in 1837 and in the 1841 census was listed as a clerk. During the period that the family stayed in Edinburgh the major influence on George McCorquodale was Alexander Cowan (1775-1859). The Cowan family of Penicuik, just a few miles south of Edinburgh, had been established as papermakers for over 60 years and were cousins of the McCorquodales through marriage. Lucia Hall's eldest sister, Elizabeth, married Alexander Cowan in 1800 and a generation before there was another marriage link. Over the previous decades the Cowan family had built a small empire surrounding their factory and increased the population of the small township of Penicuik threefold. The head of the firm, Alexander Cowan, was a successful business man but also became known as a benevolent and public spirited works owner. It was reported after his death that he had given half of his wealth away in philanthropic causes. He must have influenced and encouraged the young George McCorquodale and there is even a possibility that George worked for him. The family story says that the Cowans encouraged him and even loaned him money to set up in printing on the pretext that they could sell him paper. But George McCorquodale was always in charge of his own destiny, he was never a slave to family or associates. At that point in time George had reached one of the great crossroads in his life. All the pieces were in place. The admiration of his father, the interruption of his education, the apprenticeship at the printers, the influence of Alexander Cowan and the offer of money had forged his personality. However working in Scotland was not enough for George McCorquodale. Within twelve months he had moved back to his roots in Liverpool, setting up as a stationer and account book manufacturer.

His first premises in Liverpool were at No.3 Orange Court, Castle Street. He had moved there from Scotland and set up business between the years of 1841 and 1843. In Castle Street there were 4 courts, branching off from the street at right angles – Slater Court, between 5 and 7 Castle Street, Swift Court, between 11 and 13 Castle Street, Union Court, between 27 and 29 Castle Street and Orange Court, between 43 and 45 Castle Street. It was an area of small businesses. Union Court has survived until the present day and gives a clear indication of a narrow, claustrophobic alley, a Dickensian vision, full of people rushing about their work.

His neighbours in the close confines of Orange Court were; at No.2 Thomas Smith, a bookbinder and the Anderton Carrying Company; at No.4 a group of people consisting of 4 Merchants: Thomas Froste, James Graham & Co., Graham, Maclean & Co., Robert Kelley. Also in the building was a Barrister, Benson Blundell and attorneys, Forshaw & Blundell. In No.8 there was William Greame & Co., a Wool Broker and Robert Still, a merchant.

Castle Street, Liverpool

The courts in Liverpool had a terrible reputation for squalor, poverty, overcrowding etc – but these were a type of business district – i.e. a small business park of the day! In Castle Street they were in an ideal position, only yards away from the Town Hall and right in the centre of the expanding city.

By 1843 George McCorquodale was firmly in place at No.3 Orange Court as a stationer and account book manufacturer. At that time he was living at 117 Duke Street. Between 1843 and 1844 George moved his residence to Falkner Street, in one of the great Georgian Terraces that survive until today.

24

On the marriage front he must have been courting a young lady because on the 24th December 1844 George McCorquodale married Louisa Kate Honan at St. Bride's, Liverpool. Present at the wedding were George Nash Gardiner, a Merchant and John Cowan, George's cousin. The church is an impressive, classical style building even today, bounded on three sides by Catherine Street, Percy Street and Huskisson Street. The marriage certificate shows George living in Falkner Street and Louisa living in Falkner Terrace. Both of their fathers are listed as Esquires. His new wife's father, Frederick Honan, came from Limerick in Ireland. He was also a successful Liverpool Merchant and by 1848 was resident in what had become the fashionable area of Toxteth Park.

St Bride's Church, Liverpool

George and Louisa Kate McCorquodale must have been a very close and passionate couple. Over the next 21 years they produced 12 children. Hugh (b.1845), Mary (b.1846), Lucia Hall (b.1848), Louisa (b.1850), Helen (b.1852), George Frederick (b.1853), Elizabeth (b.1855), Alexander Cowan (b.1858), Kate (b.1860), Isabella Best (b.1862), Norman (b.1863) and Harold (b.1865). All but one of them reached adulthood. On the whole they followed the tradition of naming children after forebears – but having so many they did at least experiment slightly.

By 1845 the Liverpool directory showed that George had moved his shop across the road to 38 Castle Street. It was a larger building in a more prominent position on the corner of Castle Street and Brunswick Street. His home address was given as Laurel cottage, 47 Smithdown Lane but he then moved to Sandon Street to allow his father to move into Laurel Cottage. Also at the same time he changed the title of his business to stationer and printer. His move to the new premises enabled him to install printing machinery, which required a larger floor space than was available in Orange Court. The addition of printing was a natural progression from the work in which he was already involved. Family sources also say that there was a business connection between the Cowan family, George McCorquodale and James Cropper, a paper maker at Burneside and Cowan Head in Cumbria. It began as far back as 1844 and in 1852 the company was owned by James Cropper, George McCorquodale and William T. Blacklock. The association between Cropper and McCorquodale carried on until well into the 20th century. It proved to be a classic and profitable combination of paper maker and printer. Cropper & Co. still produce speciality paper today. It must be said that George in 1845 could be satisfied with his achievements in Liverpool. He had a successful company, a good house and an expanding family. But that was not enough. His ambitions grew and within five years he had expanded his printing company countrywide.

The London & North Western Railway

The year of 1846 was the great dramatic year in which everything changed for George McCorquodale, the stationer and printer of Castle Street, Liverpool. He managed, in partnership with William Thomas Blacklock of Manchester, to obtain the complete printing business of the London & North Western Railway. The L&NWR was a major railway company that had been created by the merger of The Grand Junction Railway, The London & Birmingham Railway and The Manchester and Birmingham Railway. It was established because of the increasing threat of the Great Western Railway against smaller railway companies. The company was formed on 16th July 1846 and the partnership of Blacklock and McCorquodale was its first printers. It was said at the time and since that the directors of the L&NWR had seen or viewed some of the printing work produced by George McCorquodale and that was why he gained the contract. However another factor was that he had allied himself with William Thomas Blacklock, an established printer of some repute. That must have gone a long way in influencing the directors of the new company. Also at this time George made the major decision to set up a completely new works at Newton probably because of the new contract.

It was reported in a local newspaper in the following way:-

"The capacious building at Newton, on the north side of the Liverpool and Manchester Railway, known as the 'Legh Arms Hotel' is being converted into a general printing office. A printing office in a village like Newton, however humble in pretension, a year ago would have been considered one of the greatest wonders of the age. Wonders do, however, occasionally appear, and one of the greatest we know of is the conversion in such a place, or of the printers to her Majesty, into a place for pressmen and printer's devils. The fact, however, is that the London and North Western Railway Company, among other amalgamations and consolidations, have contracted with a practical person to undertake this department exclusively; and the house in question has been selected as the best adapted for the purpose, all things considered, upon any portion of their lengthened territory."

The Old Conservative Hall Newton

It must have appeared as a very bold move by George McCorquodale when he took such a major step and set up on a completely new site in the seemingly backwater town of Newton. However there were a number of extenuating circumstances related to the decision. Newton or Newton-in-Makerfield or Newton-le-Willows as it became known was at the centre both of the country and of the rapidly expanding railway network.

The newly formed London & North Western Railway joined the Liverpool & Manchester Railway at what was termed Warrington Junction, just a mile from the new factory. It was later known as Newton Junction and then became Earlestown Station. The premises that he had purchased was the South Lancashire Conservative Hall, an impressive Greek style building that had fallen into disuse. It was built in 1835 for the prime reason of generating more interest in the local Tory cause but had been hardly used. The hall was available for conversion and it was within a few yards of Newton railway station. The building was capacious and could be easily converted into a works to accommodate all the large machinery associated with printing. The local lords of the manor, the Legh family of Lyme Park, were progressive landowners and open to the development and improvement of their property. Also Newton itself at that time had become a railway town, changing from a sleepy village to an industrial centre in a matter of a few decades. It suited George McCorquodale down to the ground. There was space to expand and he was on the railway network that provided most of his business.

Also linked with the move to Newton was the setting up of the London branch at Cardington Street. George McCorquodale travelled with the directors of the L&NWR on the first ever through train from Liverpool to London and arranged for a small printing office to be installed in a building adjacent to the Doric Arch at Euston Station. Before the year 1851 premises under the management of Mr. E. Eginton were in operation in Cardington Street immediately adjacent to Euston Station. There was also a Euston Stationery Office operating from the same address under Mr. R. Hilton, who was the representative in contact with the railway company. The staff consisted of the Manager, a Manager's Assistant, 7 Compositors, 3 Machine men, 2 Press men, 1 Ruler, 1 Sewer, 2 Bookbinders, 1 Messenger, 1 Warehouseman and 3 Apprentices. The total wage bill was £26 : 11s : 4d. They had 6 main customers: L&NWR, South Eastern Railway, Bucks Railway, Railway Clearing House, Chester & Holyhead Railway and East & West India Docks Railway. The original factory in Cardington Street was a private house with a workshop at the rear. The area was mostly furniture workshops and these were one by one taken over by the company and connected to the new factory.

Within twelve months George McCorquodale had also moved his family to Newton. He took up residence in the Parsonage House immediately behind the local church of St Peter and a short distance from his new works and the railway station. Previously Peter Legh, the local vicar and brother of Thomas Legh the Lord of the Manor, lived there. In the future Thomas Legh would go a long way to improve his Newton estates, even damming the local brook to produce Newton Lake. His idea was to surround it with villa residences for local industrialists. The lake adjoined the home of George McCorquodale. George and Kate raised their large family at the Parsonage, later renaming it The Willows. The Newton story about their children states that one day on coming home from a business trip George found to his horror all his children playing on the ice on Newton Lake. The incident resulted in George building a skating rink in the garden of his house. It is still there today, hidden amongst the shrubbery.

The front door to The Willows, Newton – 1930s

It was about that time that the firm of McCorquodale became involved in the early life of a future famous artist. Frederic Shields (1833-1911) was a British artist, illustrator and designer closely associated with Manchester. During his career he was influenced by Dante Gabriel Rossetti, Ford Madox Brown and William Blake. His most important legacy is the stained glass designs in Eaton Hall in Cheshire, St Elizabeth's Church in Stockport and the Chapel of the Ascension, Bayswater Road, London. His father, John, was a foreman bookbinder employed at McCorquodales in the late 1840s at their Newton works.

Frederic at that time was living and studying in London as an apprentice without pay to a firm of lithographers. His father sent for him and got him some part time work at Newton colouring in posters and other odd jobs. Frederic's spare time was taken up by sketching local scenes and people. John Shields returned to London in 1849 due to ill health but he got his son a permanent job in Manchester at a lithographers. Frederic was out of work for a while when the firm he was working for failed and he suffered quite a bit of hardship before being employed by Bradshaw & Blacklock for seven shillings a week. W.T.Blacklock commissioned him to do two large drawings of the exterior and interior of McCorquodale's works at Newton for a paltry sum of seven shillings. Frederic complained that he had not a fragment of food during the work. He later took to sketching faces at the Newton factory for 7 shillings each to alleviate his poverty. Frederic was also commissioned to do some views of London which were incorporated into a guide book entitled: "Bradshaw's Guide through London and its Environs." It was printed by McCorquodales in the Great Exhibition year of 1851. After severing his connections with the local printing industry Frederic Shields went on to be acknowledged as a great artist and illustrator.

George's partner, William T. Blacklock was also part of Bradshaw & Blacklock of Manchester. The company was started by George Bradshaw around 1830 and William Blacklock was employed as an apprentice in 1831. William must have impressed George Bradshaw because he made him a partner at the young age of 21. The firm later took on his brother, Henry Blacklock, also an engraver and printer. The company became famous for the celebrated Bradshaw's Railway Guides – known from the TV programmes of today. William Blacklock, who was born in 1817 the same year as George McCorquodale, was also director and largest shareholder in the Lancashire & Yorkshire Railway and played a prominent part in the various charitable institutions of Manchester. In 1850 the company of Bradshaw & Blacklock purchased a licence from George Baxter, the colour printer, to produce what was known as Baxter Prints. George Baxter was a colour picture printer who had invented a process that brought decorative colour prints to ordinary people.

George Bradshaw died in 1853 while travelling abroad on company business but the two brothers carried on under the name of Bradshaw & Blacklock. William T. Blacklock supposedly retired from the business in 1857 but records show he was still in partnership with his brother as late as 1863. In 1870 William Blacklock at the young age of 53 died suddenly, actually on the morning of the wedding of his second daughter. It is possible that at time the company changed its name to Henry Blacklock & Co. Henry only survived his brother for fourteen months dying possibly in the same way in 1871 at the age of 52. Henry's will, dated 21st September 1871, made George McCorquodale and Henry Fairbrother, both termed printers, the executors. The partnership between McCorquodale and Henry Blacklock & Co carried on and they published the various Railway Guides in conjunction at both works in Newton and Manchester. The firm of Henry Blacklock & Co later became part of the McCorquodale group and survived until the end of the parent company in the 20th century.

In the 1851 census George McCorquodale was shown as settled at the Parsonage House with his wife Louisa Kate and their first four children, Hugh, Mary, Lucia Hall and Louisa. They had 3 live-in staff consisting of Cook, Nurse and Housemaid. His profession was a Stationer, Printer and Master of two firms. He employed 63 men, 33 boys, 27 women and 14 girls. The 1851 census also showed that his sisters Elizabeth and Helen had moved to Newton as well. None of his sisters married and all at some time were resident in Newton.

The census of that year also gave a good insight into the new workforce at the Newton factory. People had come from all over the country to work at McCorquodales. Places such as Sheffield, Shrewsbury, Manchester, Derby, Bristol and London are all mentioned in the returns. Ireland was well represented but the biggest contribution was from Scotland. George always appreciated the hard work and endeavour of his fellow Scots, employing them whenever he could. Local speech must have developed a definite Scottish ring to it at that time because, as well as McCorquodales, other firms in Newton were taking on large numbers of Scottish tradesmen. The works also provided employment for the young people of the Newton area mostly children of Newton inhabitants.

Newton in 1851 was split into distinctive areas with employees living near to the relevant works. The township had attracted quite a number of industrial units such as the Vulcan works, the Crown Glass works, the Chemical works and the Viaduct works all closely surrounded by their own employees. The McCorquodale workers congregated in the High Street, Church Street, Mill Street (soon to be Mill Lane) and Coal Pit Lane areas. Many of them were lodgers probably having just moving to the district. Alice Houghton, who lived on Coal Pit Lane (Ashton Road), had two of her sons at the works. The two boys, George and Henry, aged 16 and 14, were assistants to bookbinders and paper machine rulers. Patrick Honohan, the Clerk and Stationer from Ireland, had both his sister Margaret and brother James at the works. James Glave, a local labourer, had 3 sons, William, Robert and Abraham gainfully employed at McCorquodales. A few yards from the works on Mill Lane Ann Arnold, who classed herself as a Landed Proprietor, had her niece Margaret working as a bookfolder and sewer. Also in her household she had 3 lodgers, John Struthey from Scotland and Thomas Kilkenny and William Ferry from Ireland all working as Printer Press Men. The ages of the children employed at the works ranged between 11 and 16. They were mostly used for envelope, folding and sewing work.

STOUR VALLEY RAILWAY.

TRAINS from WOLVERHAMPTON. [December, 1853.

An early type of timetable by McCorquodale

M'CORQUODALE AND CO., PRINTERS, LONDON.—WORKS, NEWTON.

The first manager at Newton was William Nicholson Shaw who lived on the High Street close to the Police Station and Market House. He came from Kingston in Surrey and would be the manager for a number of years. In the early 1850s William Shaw moved to Cardington Street to take charge of the growing business in the capital. George Hilton succeeded him at the relatively young age of 24. He had been an apprentice at the Newton works and must have impressed George McCorquodale to rise to manager at such an early age. He came from Shrewsbury, married a Newton girl and lived for many years at Willow Bank a large house adjacent to the works. George Hilton would be manager at Newton for the next 28 years. Willow Bank became the recognised building for the managers of the Newton works for well over a hundred years.

[No. XVI.]   3ᴿᴰ Mo. (MARCH,) 1843.   [PRICE 6D.

BRADSHAW'S

MONTHLY

GENERAL RAILWAY AND STEAM NAVIGATION

GUIDE,

FOR GREAT BRITAIN AND IRELAND,

CONTAINING A CORRECT ACCOUNT OF THE HOURS OF DEPARTURE OF THE TRAINS ON EVERY RAILWAY IN GREAT BRITAIN & IRELAND;

WITH A MAP OF THE RAILWAYS

IN THE COUNTIES OF WILTS, SOMERSET, AND GLAMORGAN,

WITH PARTS OF THE RAILWAYS IN THE COUNTIES OF

GLOUCESTER, BERKS, HANTS, & DEVON,

AND

LIST OF SHARES;

EXHIBITING AT ONE VIEW THE COST, TRAFFIC, LENGTH, DIVIDEND, AND MARKET VALUE OF THE SAME, UP TO THE END OF EACH MONTH:

THE

DEPARTURE OF HER MAJESTY'S MAILS,

AND

BRITISH AND FOREIGN STEAM VESSELS;

WITH A

LIST OF PLACES, &c. TO WHICH TRAVELLERS AND VOYAGERS RESORT, WITH EVERY USEFUL INFORMATION BOTH MERCANTILE AND OTHERWISE.

London:

PUBLISHED AT BRADSHAW'S RAILWAY INFORMATION OFFICE, 50, FLEET-STREET, W J. ADAMS, AGENT.

To whom Advertisements and Communications may be sent;

AND SOLD BY

ALL BOOKSELLERS AND RAILWAY COMPANIES.

A title page from one of the famous Bradshaw Guides

The Whirlwind

Throughout the 1850s there was a veritable whirlwind of activity surrounding George McCorquodale. George and his family were settled in their new home and the Newton works was becoming the centre of his operations. He consolidated his holdings in the Newton area in 1854 by leasing the old Legh Arms Hotel, a building adjacent to the old Conservative Hall and next to the railway. The Legh Arms Hotel had been constructed by Thomas Legh the lord of the manor in 1830 after the construction of the Liverpool and Manchester Railway. His idea was to provide a stopping off point for travellers on the new railway, mid-way between Manchester and Liverpool, similar to the stagecoach service. Thomas Legh did not realise that the improvement of the power and speed of the new locomotives made that idea redundant almost immediately. In 1851 it was being run by William Clarke from Yorkshire who classed himself as a Hotel Keeper. He and his wife Mary had four live-in staff and the cook lived next door in the railway lodge. In the census the guests were a Civil Engineer, an Officer of the Inland Revenue and a Lady travelling on her own with her son and one servant. However the hotel was never a complete success and was always regarded as a white elephant. George McCorquodale saw the Legh Arms Hotel as a perfect addition to his Newton works. In 1852 he made an offer for the building but it was refused as insufficient by William Mercer, the estate manager for the Legh family. He improved his offer and finally gained control of the building in 1854.

In the same year Thomas Legh had decided to construct another hotel of the same name in front of the station directly on the main road that ran through the township. George McCorquodale connected the Legh Arms and the old Conservative Hall together and used the hotel as the print office. He also leased other land in the immediate area to amalgamate the two buildings. George was fortunate with the position of the works which had a direct access to the railway network and to a major road linking the local towns.

The Old Legh Arms Hotel
Newton

Between the years of 1850 and 1860 George McCorquodale also greatly expanded his influence in London. The Post Office London Directory for 1852 showed:-

"McCorquodale, George & Co. railway printers, 24 Cardington Street, Hampstead Road, & printing & stationery works, Newton, Lancashire, warehouse, 38 Castle Street, Liverpool."

There were already a number of well established printers in London and he would be competing with them a long way from his works in Newton. Within twenty years he had printing works, offices and warehouses in Cardington Street, St. Thomas' Street (The Armoury), Coleman Street, Duke Street and Change Alley – all properties situated in London.

The Armoury in St Thomas' Street was the biggest investment in London; it covered Nos. 64, 66 and 68. The building could have been an armoury and was possibly purchased cheaply by George McCorquodale. Photographs in the next century show a large number of rooms with low ceilings supported by cast iron pillars, typical of a strongly built storage facility. There is a possibility that it was a nickname used by the print workers because in reality the area was dominated by large hop warehouses in the vicinity of the Hop Exchange in Southwark Street, London. The advantage of the building was that it was close to London Bridge and Waterloo railway stations so was ideal for George's purposes. Another shrewd move was acquiring premises in Coleman Street right in the centre of the commercial district of the city. It was situated between the Guildhall and the Bank of England building at the very heart of the business district. Coleman Street was initially known for producing calculators but later became the main offices for McCorquodale & Co. Ltd. It was to be the main office well into the 20th Century, before being moved to the more impressive King Street nearby. Change Alley was very close to Coleman Street and was probably used as a small retail premises serving the large local business area. The alley has survived until the present day and was similar in shape and character to Orange Court in Liverpool. Only a few years after the London venture George was at the other end of the country, opening up offices in Glasgow. The Glasgow Directory for 1854 showed the following:-

"McCorquodale & Co., railway & general printers, paper rulers, and Bookbinders, 32 Dunlop Street and 40 St Enoch Wynd."

The first manager at Glasgow was William Fletcher. He had worked for the company since 1852 and had been transferred from London when the McCorquodale company was being set up in Glasgow.

One of the oldest surviving pieces of
McCorquodale printing. It is the company
stamp on the inside of an account book dated 1856.
The account book was produced for
Richard Evans & Co. of Haydock,
a local coal company.
The first pages have the watermark
GEO. McCORQUODALE LIVERPOOL 1856.
The rest of the pages are by J. TOWN,
TURKEY MILL, 1848

RULES

TO BE OBSERVED BY THE

COLLIERS AND OTHER WORKERS

AT THE

HAYDOCK,

ASHTON, PARR, AND EDGE GREEN

COLLIERIES.

M'CORQUODALE & CO., PRINTERS, LONDON:
WORKS, NEWTON.
1865.

A small booklet produced by
McCorquodale for
Richard Evans & Co.,
Haydock.
It is a list of rules and
regulations for colliers

The story was related years later by William Foote, the manager in the 1890s:-

"We bought the plant and stock from Mr. John Neilson, who wanted to give up the business. When Mr. McCorquodale came to Glasgow for the final negotiations, we paid as near as I can recollect between £900 and £1000 for the business. It was a small flat and attic in Dunlop Street opposite the old Theatre Royal. Soon we had another flat in St. Enoch Wynd, near Maxwell Street. There we installed our first printing machine, which was driven by steam power from one of our neighbours, and the inventor came to Glasgow to fit it up. After a short time, the increase of business forced us to look for bigger premises. And these we found in Havelock Buildings, opposite '96' where we thought we would have a long rest. But increasing business kept pushing us out and we had to purchase a site in Maxwell Street – and there we erected the small, low building, in which are our present offices."

Later they purchased other buildings in the area and within two years the company had established itself in the area that became the Glasgow home of the company, 96 Maxwell Street. It later became known as the Caxton Works. The building still survives today. It is on the Scotland 'Buildings under risk' register because it is of note and still retains its unusual tiled exterior. Of late the building is quite run down being in the area of the Glasgow lap dancing scene.

In 1864 the Liverpool side of the business was converted into a limited company with the title of The Liverpool Printing & Stationery Company. The directors were mostly comprised of managers but there was still an ongoing McCorquodale family involvement on the board. In 1870 another venture attracted George McCorquodale. With the aid of his son-in-law Charles Edward Hamilton, he set up a paper making business in North Wales. George knew the paper business because as early as the 1850s he was producing paper in Liverpool. The North Wales Paper Co. Ltd., as the company became known, was set up in Oakenholt, Flint. Here there were railway facilities and a plentiful supply of good water. Production started in 1871 and in 1880 a further paper machine was added doubling output. At first the business specialised in the production of news, white and coloured paper. Then, towards the end of the century, a better class of product was manufactured. In 1891 the works was further expanded when the company installed plant for producing caustic soda in an attempt to undercut the Alkali Union which was holding prices high. The works was part of McCorquodales well into the 1960s.

A Victorian printing machine advertisement with a testimonial by McCorquodale

By the mid 1870s George had taken into partnership his eldest surviving son George Frederick and his son-in-law, Charles Edward Hamilton. George and his two partners had become involved in a dispute in 1876 regarding the winding up of The London and Provincial Illustrated Newspaper Company. The Chancery Court named the three of them as partners in McCorquodale & Co. The work that the company was doing in London was rewarded on the 8th of February 1876 when George McCorquodale and his son George Frederick McCorquodale were given the accolade of Freedom of the City. They were introduced by the Company of Spectacle Makers. In 1880 George McCorquodale turned the business into a Private Limited Liability Company with the Registered Office at Cardington Street where it remained until it was transferred to Coleman Street in the twentieth century.

[AMENDED BILL.]

London and North Western Railway.

RETURNED EMPTIES BY PASSENGER TRAINS.

The following Scale of Charges for the conveyance by Passenger Trains of ALL RETURNED EMPTIES, with the exception of MILK CANS, is in operation:—

Not exceeding 25 miles ... ... 2d. each package.
Above 25 and not exceeding 75 miles 4d. ,, ,,
,, 75 ,, ,, 150 ,, 6d. ,, ,,
,, 150 ,, ,, 250 ,, 9d. ,, ,,
Any distance above 250 ,, 1s. ,, ,,

Maximum charge to be 1s., and full Parcels Rates to be paid in cases where the packages shall not, in the first instance, have been sent by Passenger Trains.

Weight of Returned Empties by Passenger Trains to be limited to half-a-hundred weight.

Fish empties *in bulk*, and returned empty Coffin Cases, are not to be conveyed by Passenger Train.

The charges in all cases to be prepaid, and booking fees will be charged in addition in London, and other places where the same are usually in operation.

RETURNED MILK CANS only will be carried free.

By Order,
W. CAWKWELL,
General Manager.

EUSTON STATION.
July, 1872.

Should this Book be lost, Two Shillings and Sixpence will be paid on its delivery at the Branch Office, Euston Station.

HORNE & CHAPLIN,
PROPRIETORS.

No. 20181.

LONDON.

When ordering Books similar to this, it will be sufficient to send the above No. and Date.

M'CORQUODALE & CO.,
RAILWAY PRINTERS AND STATIONERS,
LONDON, NEWTON, LIVERPOOL, AND GLASGOW.

A London & North Western Account Book by McCorquodale. Note the title – Railway Printers and Stationers

Later In the century further expansion was made over the Pennines into the city of Leeds. Initially in 1872 they were positioned in Baines' Buildings in Bank Street, Leeds under the title of Printers, Stationers, Lithographers, Engravers and Account Book Manufacturers. The Leeds works was known for lithography or high grade printing as well as engraving. When the Leeds branch was opened the staff and plant of the Lithographic Department were transferred from Newton. Within 20 years the works had settled in bigger premises at Gutenberg Buildings, Basinghall Street in the centre of Leeds. By the 1880s the Leeds enterprise had extended to such an extent that it was one of the largest establishments in the town.

Other smaller premises were opened in various parts of the country such as Birmingham, in the Cobden Buildings, Corporation Street and in Cardiff at Mount-Stuart Square near to the docks. The Cardiff office was opened because of the large number of Welsh railways with which they dealt.

41

The story of the Wolverton works in Buckinghamshire began with a request. Sir Richard Moon, Chairman of the London & North Western Railway was concerned about the employment of young women in Wolverton. The town was predominantly a railway town and had been closely linked with the London North Western Railway for many years. Wolverton was at the centre of the old London & Birmingham Railway and had been set up as a railway workshop and stores. The situation in the 1870s was that, although the majority of the men were employed, there was little for the women of the township to do. Sir Richard made contact with his friend and associate George McCorquodale and requested that he provide some sort of employment in the township. They had known each other and worked together for many years on the printing business of L.&N.W.R. countrywide. George agreed to his suggestion and by 1878 he had opened a works primarily based on the production of registered envelopes. The works rapidly increased in size and diversified into other forms of printing & stationery. By the 1880s the Wolverton works employed 120 women and 20 men - but the factory was not just cheap labour for young women. The company provided the best welfare and working facilities in the area. The staff had dining, reading and recreation rooms on site. Girls were encouraged to stay as long as possible and wedding grants, pension funds and bonuses were set up to ease the burden of the long hours they worked. It was a typical McCorquodale enterprise proving that if you look after your workforce they will look after you.

NORTH WESTERN HOTEL LIME STREET STATION LIVERPOOL
LONDON & NORTH WESTERN RAILWAY

LONDON (EUSTON SQUARE) THE EUSTON HOTEL
LONDON & NORTH WESTERN RAILWAY

Hotel advertisements from McCorquodale timetables about 1880.
Top – Liverpool Lime Street.
Bottom – London Euston

Family

Family life for the McCorquodales at Newton was not without tragedy. They were extremely lucky that all but one of their children reached maturity. Lucia Hall died in 1853 at the age of 5. A more serious event struck the family in 1868 when their eldest son Hugh died at the young age of 23. J.H.Lane in his History of Newton in Makerfield related the sad story:-

"In the third year of our Apprenticeship an event occurred in Newton that made a profound impression on the inhabitants- the death of Mr. Hugh McCorquodale, upon the 31st January, 1868, in his twenty third year. Only two years previously great rejoicings had been witnessed at his coming of age, festivities on a large scale had taken place at the Works, with presentations from the employees and addresses of Congratulation by the different heads of the departments, and an announcement had been made by his father that his eldest son Hugh had become a partner in the firm. And now the alarming news went through the Works that he was stricken with rheumatism of the heart and was not likely to recover; and then, a little later, that he had passed away. We well remember the consternation this event produced both in the Works and in the village – that he, a young man of fine physique and foremost in every sport in the place, should be struck down so prematurely! He was a regular communicant at St Peter's, a Sunday-school teacher, an intimate friend of our late Vicar, a captain of the Volunteers, the captain of the rowing-team at the lake, and was generally associated with every movement for the enlightenment and recreation of the youth of the neighbourhood."

The above stated agreement for accepting Hugh as a Partner in the firm was signed by W.T.Blacklock and George McCorquodale showing the two men's close affiliation still existed in 1866. One amusing anecdote about Hugh was that when he became of age he was presented with a large piece of oriental pottery, which he proceeded to drop due to the effects of consuming too much alcohol at the party. The family story regarding the death of Hugh McCorquodale was that he developed pneumonia after a severe drenching whilst out riding and refused to change into dry clothes. The sudden demise of Hugh was used as a warning to future McCorquodale children regarding getting changed out of wet clothes!

J.H. Lane was taken on as an apprentice by McCorquodales, with the kind aid of young Hugh McCorquodale. J. H. Lane related the story:-

'The boys or girls who attend Sunday school are more likely to get on well in the world than those who stay away and receive little or no religious instruction. Masters prefer to have boys recommended by their day school or Sunday school teachers rather than those who cannot get such recommendation. I will tell you a story to illustrate this, and also to mention a good turn that was once done to me by the young Mr. McCorquodale whose name is in your prizes. When I had attained the manly age of fourteen, my parents thought it time I commenced to learn a Trade. I heard there was a vacancy for an apprentice in the composing room of the printing office; so, one morning, I went to McCorquodale's Works to see if I could get a job. I mounted that long flight of stone steps to the clerk's offices, opened the door, and walked in. Just as I entered, Mr. Hugh McCorquodale was passing, and, seeing me, said, "Well Lane, what do you want?" I said I wanted to be an apprentice in the composing room. "Very well; come along with me!" He led me down some steps to a long narrow office, at one end of which sat a grey headed old gentleman wearing a snuff coloured wig. His surname was Barclay. He looked down on me, and said in a kind voice, "Well, my little mannie, what do you want?" "Please, sir, I want to be a compositor!" "Oh! Can you read?" Before I could answer, Mr. Hugh said, "Oh, yes! He can read; I have heard him often at the Sunday school." "I should like to hear you read, my little mannie," said Mr. Barclay, and he handed me a newspaper. I read part of the leading article, and he told me to start the next Monday morning at eight o'clock.'

That was the beginning of J.H. Lane's career in printing and publishing. The story of John Henry Lane and his friend Peter Mayor Campbell was closely linked to the history of McCorquodale and the town of Newton itself. The Lane family came to Newton because of the close association of John Lane, the father of J.H.Lane, and Thomas Legh. John Lane, who came from the Isle of Wight, was engaged as mate on the yacht of Thomas Legh for a number of years. Subsequently, due to the ill health of Thomas Legh, he was invited to become the keeper of Newton Mere and so the family moved north. Peter Mayor Campbell was born in Ayrshire in Scotland and came with his father to work at a tilery at Newton for Thomas Legh. The two young men, John Henry Lane and Peter Mayor Campbell, were apprentices at McCorquodale in Newton and Blacklocks in Manchester. During their career they worked on proof reading for the Bradshaw's Guide for many years. John Henry Lane became a small printer in his own right and produced, with aid of his friend Peter Mayor Campbell, two fine volumes on the History of Newton-in-Makerfield.

It was in his book on Newton that J.H.Lane related the story of the disastrous fire that occurred at the Newton works:-

"The print works were brought prominently to our notice during our schoolboy days, when in the early hours of the morning of the 16th February 1865, the whole of the village was awakened from its slumber by the clanging of bells at the works, the church, and the schools; by the cry of 'FIRE!' from a hundred throats, and by the tramping of many feet hurrying towards the scene of the conflagration. The fire began in the hotel portion of the works, and immediate steps were taken to cut off the communication between this and the machine department in the old Conservative Hall. This was ultimately effected by destroying the gangway connecting the two establishments and by barricading the doorways with reams of paper. The only machines destroyed were a few used in the envelope making and paper-ruling rooms. The extensive stock of paper filling the other parts of the premises was completely destroyed, the building was gutted, and the walls were left roofless and ready to fall. However, rebuilding operations were immediately begun, the damage was repaired, and the works were soon in full activity."

One good thing that came out of the fire was that they were able to remodel the interior of the building to make it more efficient.

George McCorquodale. He was never without a small flower and a sprig of heather in his buttonhole

By the 1860s and 1870s the children of George McCorquodale were growing up. They were the offspring of a successful business man and were certainly moving in wealthy circles. Therefore when it came to marriage they had wide choice of prospective partners   The first of them to marry was Mary to Charles Edward Hamilton in 1867. He must have impressed his father-in-law because within a few years he was made a director of the company. Charles was the son of John Hamilton, a Liverpool merchant born in Scotland and living at Huskisson Street, Liverpool. The next to marry, in 1871, was Louisa to Henry Sherlock, vicar of St. James' in Haydock. He was vicar there in 1878 when over two hundred men and boys lost their lives at Wood Pit in Haydock. Henry Sherlock had to help and comfort the families of the dead and gave a sad and passionate service in the church a number of days later. Within two years he had moved to Scotland, whether it was to do with the trauma of the pit disaster it's not known. He then became vicar at Coldham in Cambridgeshire before finally settling at Bildeston in Suffolk. A few years later, in 1874, Helen married Robert Low Greenshields, a Liverpool ship owner. He was the son of John Greenshields, another of the Liverpool merchant set, who was also born in Scotland and lived at Falkner Street, Liverpool. Initially Robert and Helen lived at Toxteth Park and then moved to the Wirral, before settling in great splendour at The Beeches, Overton, Cheshire.

In 1879 there were two marriages in the McCorquodale household. The eldest of the surviving sons, George Frederick, married Mary Augusta Walcott Henderson, the daughter of Sir Edmund Yeamans Walcott Henderson, the Chief Commissioner of the Metropolitan Police. He was famous for founding the Metropolitan & City Police Orphans Fund. Then Elizabeth wed Hugh Francis Birley, the son of Joseph Hornby Birley, part owner of the Newton-le-Willows Sugar Works, who lived for some time at Brookside House in Newton. One of their children, Sir Oswald Birley, was a distinguished painter of society and royalty in the early part of the 20th century. Kate McCorquodale married twice, firstly in 1883 to William James Sinclair Blacklock, the son of William T. Blacklock, the deceased business partner of George McCorquodale. William James died suddenly in 1894 at the young age of 33. In 1897 Kate married Henry Sinclair Horne, who would distinguish himself in the 1st World War. The year 1886 saw two further marriages in the family. Alexander Cowan married Maggie Janet Cox and Isabella Best wed Joseph Hume Dudgeon. Maggie Janet Cox was the daughter of Alexander Cobb Cox, a Liverpool merchant and broker, who lived in some style at Beech Mount, Garston and like Hugh McCorquodale had come from Scotland to make his fortune. Joseph Hume Dudgeon was a stockbroker who lived and worked in Dublin, Ireland. In 1893 Harold, the youngest son, married Grace Granville, the daughter of Major Bevil Granville, keeping up the military tradition of the family. Norman, the last of the boys to marry, wed Constance Helena Burton in 1897, the daughter of Edmund Charles Burton. Norman's father-in-law, Edmund Burton, nicknamed Doughey, was town clerk and clerk to the justices in Daventry. He went to Oxford, rowed in the Boat Race and was an accomplished runner. His greatest claim to fame was his involvement with the National Hunt. He won the first National Hunt Chase Challenge Cup in 1860 on Bridegroom at Market Harborough. The race was later moved to Cheltenham where it remains to the present day. There is a grand memorial to him in Daventry market square erected by The National Hunt Committee in 1911.

The marriages of his sons and daughters proved how far George McCorquodale had risen in society and the circles in which he moved. A wonderful example of a McCorquodale wedding was reported in the Earlestown Guardian for September 1st 1883:-

"The marriage of Miss Kate McCorquodale, fifth daughter of Col. George McCorquodale, of The Willows, Newton to Mr. W.J. Sinclair Blacklock, took place on Tuesday, August 28th, 1883, at St. Peter's Church, Newton-le-Willows.

The church had been tastefully decorated. The nave, with the aisle leading to the vestry, was laid with red baize, and the footway from the road to the church covered with the same material. The communion rails were ornamented with scotch heather and moss interspersed with sweet scented jasmine. Shortly after 11 o'clock, the bride was escorted into the church by her father, Col. George McCorquodale – several children strewing the path with flowers – followed by eight bridesmaids, namely, Miss J. McCorquodale, Miss Nairne, Miss Birley, Miss Donton, Miss Hamilton, Miss L.W.K. Hamilton, Miss Edith B.E. McCorquodale and Miss Mabel Sherlock. The bridegroom was accompanied by Capt. Price, who officiated as best man. The dress worn by the bride was of white satin with a beautiful tulle veil fastened by star diamonds, the latter being the gift of the bridegroom and of Mr. G.F. McCorquodale, the bride's eldest brother. The bridesmaids wore cream lace skirts and surah top polonaises, a la Watteau, hats of the same colour, lined with salmon pink surah, pink mittens and diamond arrow brooches, the gift of the bridegroom.

The wedding ceremony was performed by the Rev. H. Monk, assisted by the Rev. H. Sherlock, of Haydock, brother-in-law of the bride. After the singing of the bridal hymns and the signing of the register, the procession was reformed and filed out of the church to the strains of Mendelsohn's 'Wedding March,' magnificently rendered by the church organist, Mr. Peter Fairclough, - the guests returned to Col. McCorquodale's residence where the 'breakfast' was spread on the veranda. There were about 70 invited guests."

It was in 1870 that George McCorquodale sadly lost his wife Kate at the young age of 47. She had suffered with chronic Bright's disease for a number of years. The term Bright's disease is not often used in the modern day but it is a form of kidney disease and very painful. That and a severe case of bronchitis, lasting over 6 weeks, caused her death on the 13th February 1870. Her children must have been devastated, the youngest being only 5 at the time of her death. They had been married for over 25 years. She was laid to rest in the family vault under the east widow of St Peter's church in Newton. With her in the vault are her eldest son, Hugh, her infant daughter, Lucia and one of her sisters-in-law, Lucia. Two years later George married his second wife Emily Sanderson at Lewes, Sussex. She was the daughter of Rev. Thomas Sanderson, Head Master of Wellingborough Grammar School and Vicar of Great Doddington, Northampton. George was nearly 55 and his bride nearly 37 at their marriage but that did not stop him beginning his second family. They had two children, Edith Beatrice Emilie in 1873 and Hugh Stewart in 1875. The two children of his second marriage had very different fates in store for them. Edith married Thomas Donnelly in 1897 and lived, on the whole, a quiet happy life but had no children. However Hugh Stewart the youngest surviving son of George McCorquodale decided to play his part for Queen and country in the Boer War. The results of that decision were related back home by none other than Winston Churchill who at that time was war correspondent for the Morning Post:-

"I will only relate one other incident, a miserable one: the day before the attack on Spion Kop I had chance to ride across the pontoon bridge. I heard my name called and saw the cheery face of a boy I had known at Harrow, a smart, clean-looking young gentleman, quite the rough material for irregular horse. He had just arrived, had pushed his way to the front, hoped, so he said, 'to get a job.' This morning they told me an unauthorised Press correspondent had been found among the killed on the summit; at least they thought at first it was a Press correspondent, for no one seemed to know him. A man had been found leaning forward on his rifle – dead. A broken pair of field glasses shattered by the same shell that had killed their owner bore the name 'McCorquodale.' The name and the face flew together in my mind. It was the last joined subaltern of Thorneycroft's Mounted Infantry – joined in the evening – shot at dawn. Poor, gallant young Englishman! He had soon 'got his job.' The great sacrifice had been required of the Queen's latest recruit."

Hugh Stewart McCorquodale had been killed by a sniper's bullet only days after reaching South Africa. He was buried with all honours on the battlefield. There were services held at both Newton and Llansadwrn churches. At Newton the service was held on February 1st 1900, when a large number of parishioners and friends plus a detachment of the 6th V. B. King's Liverpool Regiment attended. Hugh Stewart was also commemorated on the war memorial outside Earlestown Town Hall. The monument was erected in 1904 with money provided by public subscription.

WAR MEMORIAL.   EARLESTOWN

The war memorial at Earlestown.
Hugh Stewart McCorquodale's name is on the middle plaque

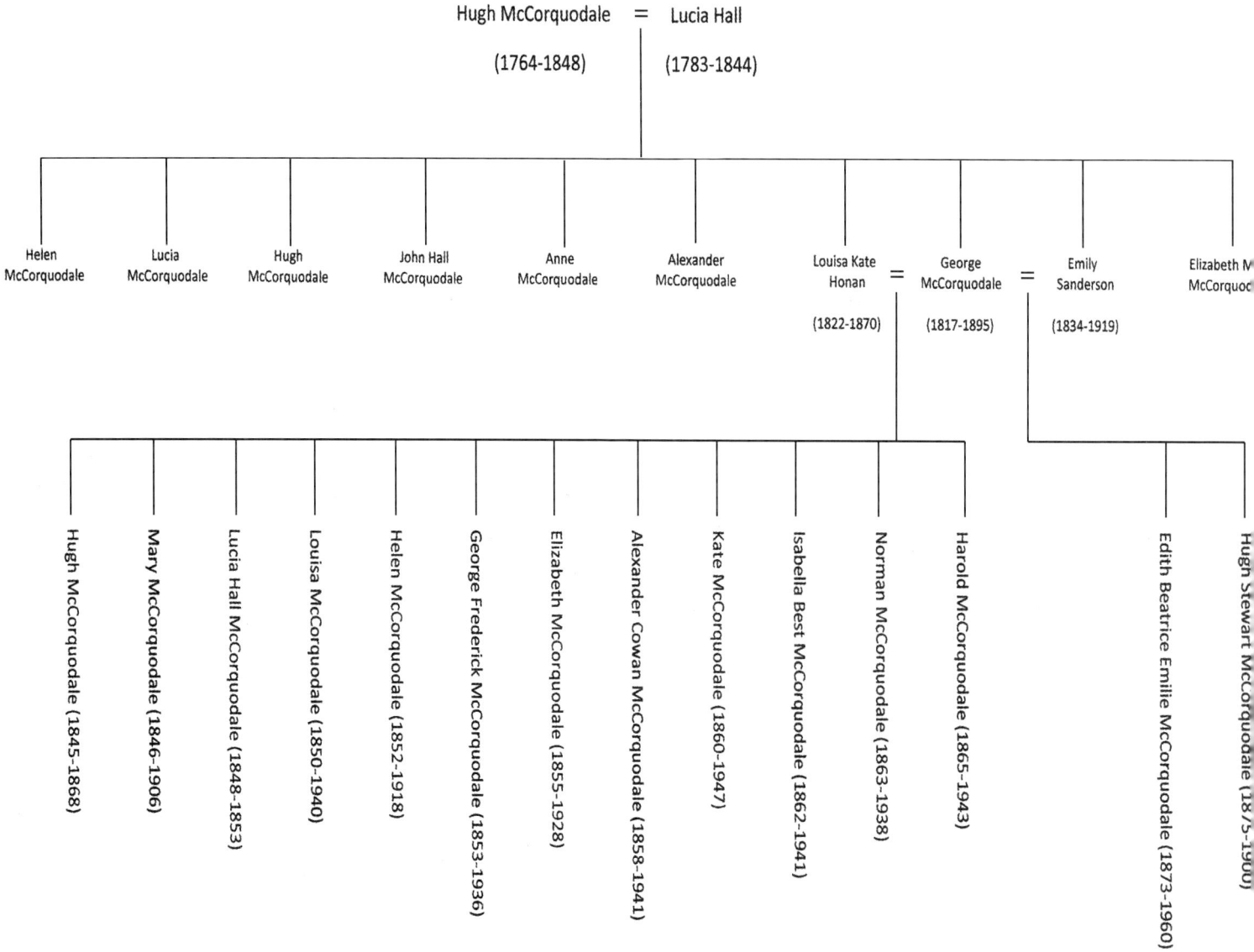

McCorquodale family tree showing immediate family of George McCorquodale

Hugh McCorquodale = Lucia Hall

(1764-1848) (1783-1844)

Helen McCorquodale

Lucia McCorquodale

Hugh McCorquodale

John Hall McCorquodale

Anne McCorquodale

Alexander McCorquodale

Louisa Kate Honan (1822-1870) = George McCorquodale (1817-1895) = Emily Sanderson (1834-1919)

Elizabeth M McCorquod

Hugh McCorquodale (1845-1868)

Mary McCorquodale (1846-1906)

Lucia Hall McCorquodale (1848-1853)

Louisa McCorquodale (1850-1940)

Helen McCorquodale (1852-1918)

George Frederick McCorquodale (1853-1936)

Elizabeth McCorquodale (1855-1928)

Alexander Cowan McCorquodale (1858-1941)

Kate McCorquodale (1860-1947)

Isabella Best McCorquodale (1862-1941)

Norman McCorquodale (1863-1938)

Harold McCorquodale (1865-1943)

Edith Beatrice Emilie McCorquodale (1873-1960)

Hugh Stewart McCorquodale (18/5-1900)

Products

The main business of McCorquodale was of course with the railway companies. The association with the London & North Western Railway was extremely profitable. The railway company was a massive and far reaching undertaking. At one time it was reputed to be the largest company in the country and riding on its shirt-tail was McCorquodale. The expertise and quality of their work resulted in them gaining a large number of contracts with other railway companies and it was said that they produced the printing work for the majority of the country's railways. By the mid 1870s McCorquodale had printing contracts with over 44 railway companies.

They consisted of:-

Colne Valley Railway
Great Western Railway
Hunstanton & West Norfolk Railway
Metropolitan Railway
Newport Pagnell Railway
Potteries, Shrewsbury & North Wales Railway
Pembroke & Tenby Railway
Rhymney Railway
Taff Vale Railway
West London Railway

Central Wales & Carmarthen Railway

Brecon & Merthyr Railway

District Railway

Aylesbury & Buckingham Railway

Wallington & Princes Risborough Railway

Furness Railway

North London Railway

West Coast Conference

West London Extension Railway

North & South West Junction Railway

Mid-Wales Railway

Irish North Western Railway

Cannock Mineral Railway

Stafford Uttoxeter Railway

East & West Junction Railway

Wolverhampton & Walsall Railway

Blyth & Tyne Railway

Cornwall & West Cornwall Railway

Hammersmith & City Railway

South Devon Railway

Lancashire & Yorkshire Railway

Bristol & Exeter Railway

Burry Port & Gwendraeth Valley Railway

Windsor & Annapolis Railway

Lancaster & Carlisle Railway

Bishops Castle Railway

Metropolitan & St. Johns Wood Railway

Northampton & Banbury Railway

Bristol Port Railway & Pier Co.

St. Austell & Pentewan Railway

Vale of Towy Joint Committee

London, Tilbury & Southend Railway

Wrexham, Mold & Connah's Quay Railway

The list contains the names of many railway companies that have completely disappeared due to later amalgamations.

An example of a Railway Gazetteer produced by McCorquodale in the 1890s.
The book itself was over 600 pages long, hard back covered and retailed for 8/6.
It listed every railway station in the country and the company that served it

FIFTY YEARS

ON THE

LONDON & NORTH WESTERN RAILWAY,

AND OTHER MEMORANDA

IN THE

LIFE OF DAVID STEVENSON.

EDITED BY LEOPOLD TURNER.

LONDON:
PRINTED BY M^cCORQUODALE & CO. LIMITED,
CARDINGTON STREET, EUSTON, N.W.

1891.

Title page of a small hardback book produced by McCorquodale, Cardington Street

A warning notice printed at the Armoury regarding the infamous Jack the Ripper

ARMOURY

An "Historical" Armoury Poster

*The first notice circularized
to householders in London's East End
during the hunt for Jack the Ripper.*

POLICE NOTICE.

TO THE OCCUPIER.

On the mornings of Friday, 31st August, Saturday 8th, and Sunday, 30th September, 1888, Women were murdered in or near Whitechapel, supposed by some one residing in the immediate neighbourhood. Should you know of any person to whom suspicion is attached, you are earnestly requested to communicate at once with the nearest Police Station.

Metropolitan Police Office,
30th September, 1888.

Printed by McCorquodale & Co. Limited, "The Armoury," Southwark.

Two books produced by
McCorquodale, Leeds

NORTH EASTERN RAILWAY

TOURIST PUBLICATIONS.

The Railway Company issue the following.

LODGING AND HOTEL GUIDE

An Illustrated Guide to Hotels and Furnished Lodgings in Seaside and Country Villages in the Counties of Northumberland, Cumberland, Westmorland, Durham, and Yorkshire; with Map. Free on application at any North Eastern Station, or by post, 2½d.

POCKET GUIDES

To "Teesdale," "The Yorkshire Coast," "Wensleydale and Swaledale," "Tynedale and the Roman Wall District," with Maps and numerous Illustrations. Price, 3d. each; by post, 4½d.

CYCLISTS' GUIDES

To North Eastern England, containing Road Maps, and numerous Illustrations. Price 3d. at bookstalls, by post, 5d.

Any of the above publications can be obtained from the Superintendent of the Line, York.

Memorandum

From Thomas Beecham,
Proprietor of Beecham's Pills.
St. Helens, Dec'r 3 1884

To Messrs McCorquodale
Newton

Dr Sirs

with respect to Printing our Hand Bills &c
I have decided to give you the order for
the printing of same for the next two
years altho I have a quotation in a
little lower than yours but knowing
you do the work well it can in
future be depended on.

We must have the first Million in
not later than Christmas.

Will you run over here and sign
the contract. or shall one of us
come over to your place. please let
us know!

Yours very resp'y
Thos Beecham

A letter from Thomas Beecham to McCorquodale & Co dated December 3rd 1884 requesting hand bills. The date is interesting because he must have trusted McCorquodales to deliver at least a million before Christmas.

Thomas Beecham was head of the St. Helens pharmaceutical firm famous for Beecham's Pills ar was a very successful entrepreneur in his own righ He was the father of Sir Thomas Beecham the we known conductor who was involved with the Londo Philharmonic and the Royal Philharmonic Orchestr

---

A London & North Western Railway poster produced by McCorquodale. It gives information on train times for Newton Races.
The event was very important and people came from far and wide to Newton Common

---

LONDON AND NORTH WESTERN RAILWAY.

NEWTON RACES.

Special Train
FROM
ST. HELENS

On FRIDAY, June 20, 1879,
At 1.10 p.m.,

Stopping to take up Passengers at PEASLEY CROSS, SUTTON OAK, and ST. HELENS JUNCTION, for

EARLESTOWN,
CLOSE TO THE RACE COURSE.
RETURNING AT 6.50 p.m.

STATIONS.	Times.	FARES.			
		First Class RETURN.	Third Class RETURN.	First Class SINGLE.	Third Class SINGLE.
	p.m.				
St. Helens	1 10	1s. 5d.	10d.	10d.	5d.
Peasley Cross ...	1 13	1s. 2d.	9d.	8d.	4½d.
Sutton Oak	1 16	1s. 2d.	8d.	8d.	4d.
St. Helens Jun.	1 20	10d.	6d.	6d.	3d.

Passengers will be Booked at EARLESTOWN by the Return Train.

Tickets and Small Bills may be obtained of the Booking Clerks at the above Stations.

All information regarding Excursion Trains on the London and North Western Railway, can be obtained on application to Mr. JAMES SHAW, District Superintendent, Lime Street Station, Liverpool.

Chief Traffic Manager's Office,
Easton Station, London, June, 1879.

G. FINDLAY.

McCorquodale & Co., Printers, London—Works Newton.

In the 1870s and 1880s the company provided the detailed timetables for the Royal train from Windsor to Ballater and back. The document has survived and provided information about the number of miles travelled, the timetable and the stations on route. The train travelled on the Great Western, the London & North Western and the Caledonian Railways. The journey covered over 590 miles, took 18 hours and passed through 240 stations. No other trains were to be allowed on the lines within 30 minutes of the Royal train. The timetable was printed at Cardington Street and also showed the arrangement of the carriages. There were two brake vans, front and rear, four 1st class carriages for men servants, pages, upper servants, dressers, ladies' maids and directors, four double saloons for other royalty and dignitaries, two royal saloons for the Queen, Princess Beatrice, personal servants and queen's dressers and a luggage truck.

Besides the railway printing work they carried out, McCorquodales branched out into other fields of printing even as early as the 1850s. Books of all types, pamphlets, posters, hand-bills were produced and long term connections were made with firms such as Richard Evans & Co., The Sankey Sugar Company and Beecham of St Helens, the famous pharmaceutical company. By the 1870s what was termed general customers numbered over 300. In London they included the East & West India Docks, The Railway Benevolent Institution, The Metropolitan Asylums Board and the Gas Light & Coke Company.

Another achievement of George McCorquodale was in the banking field when he became director of Parr's Bank of Warrington. It was founded by Joseph Parr in the 18th century and was sometimes referred to as the Warrington bank. Joseph Parr was a wealthy sugar producer whose family came from Grappenhall near Warrington. Their wealth enabled them to break into banking and they became a very successful company, finally amalgamating with the Westminster bank in the 20th century.

In 1893 a personal accolade was given to George McCorquodale when he was entered into "Liverpool's Legion of Honour" a book compiled by B. Guinness Orchard. It was a large work that listed of all the famous people connected to the city of Liverpool. Also about that time the company acquired the printing work for the national government so they were able to add that they were printers to Her Majesty's Government. That must have been a major coup for the company which secured the wealth and prestige of the family well into the 20th century.

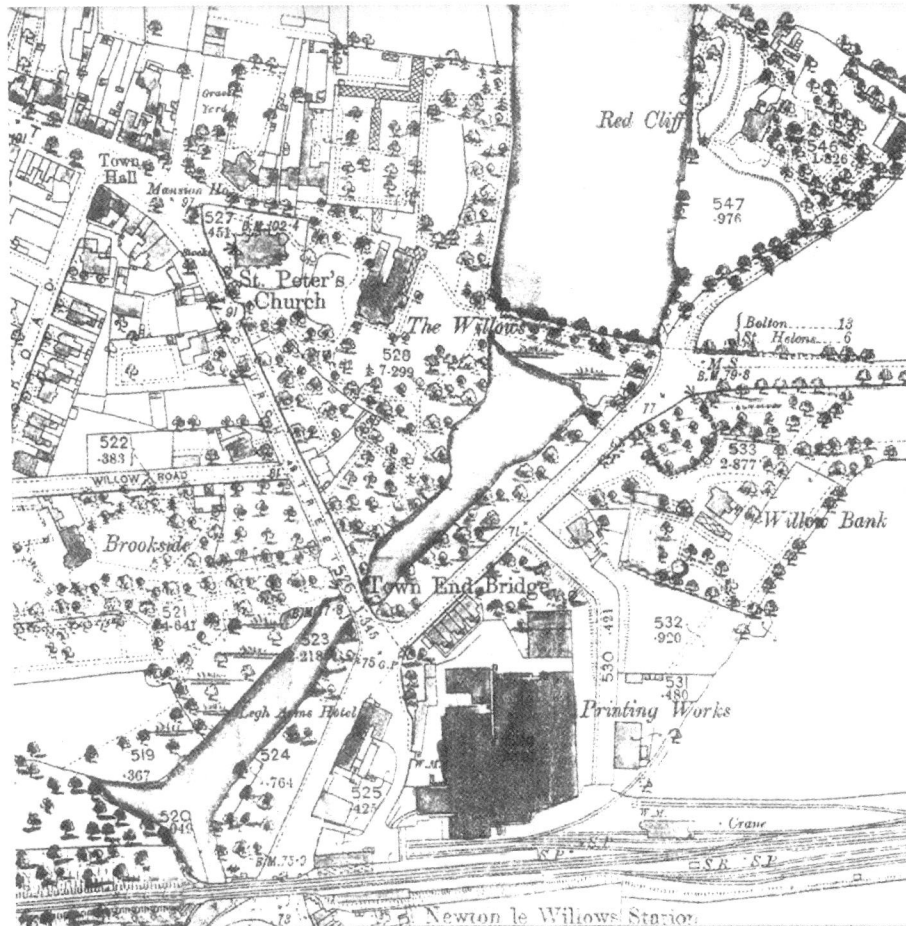

A map of Newton showing McCorquodale Printing Works, Newton Station, The Willows, St. Peter's Church and Willow Bank

Community Service

Throughout his time at Newton George McCorquodale involved himself in the local community. After his arrival he became a close friend of Peter Legh, the local vicar and supported him in his quest for better education for local children. Peter Legh was passionate about the education of ordinary children and his great achievement was the building of St Peter's Church Schools. The Legh family provided money by donations, investments and a gift of land to make the project successful. The school was opened in 1860 and 6 Trustees were appointed to oversee the facility. Their names were inscribed in the stonework over the door to the belfry. Today no belfry remains at St Peter's school but the names are still there – Peter Legh, the vicar, William John Legh, the lord of the manor, George McCorquodale, the printer, Joseph Hornby Birley, Sugar refiner and William Caunce, a local farmer. In 1864 Peter Legh retired from his work at St Peter's due to ill health. The presentation was given by George McCorquodale who spoke at length about the good work Peter Legh had done in the community. George McCorquodale's desire to be involved in the local community of Newton resulted in him being quickly made a local JP and Magistrate. He became a diligent dispenser of justice, probably thinking he was responsible for the moral upbringing of the local people.

St. Peter's School, Newton
c.1900.

George became Chairman of the Newton Petty Sessions and rarely missed attending the meetings. The local newspaper reports of the Petty Sessions showed him in the chair under his preferred title of Colonel McCorquodale support by his son, Hugh, T.J.Gillespie, a paper manufacturer from Mill Lane, Newton, Charles Bell Ford Borron, head of the local council, Robert Stone, a wealthy builder, who had constructed half of Earlestown and Colonel J.L.Wood, manager of McCorquodale's Newton works. They consisted of a powerful mix of the local dignitaries. They dispensed justice on a various number of crimes such as cruelty to animals, theft, drunkenness, unmuzzled canines and quarrelsome neighbours. Even though he was known for his good nature he was still a strict disciplinarian regarding public order.

Another of the institutions that George McCorquodale was involved in and of which he was justly proud was the local Volunteer Force. Volunteer forces had been raised in England a number of times in the past, notably around the time of Waterloo. In the late 1850s, due to unrest in parts of Europe, communities were encouraged to raise and train volunteers. Britain on the whole did not support a standing army so it was necessary. George McCorquodale was instrumental in the formation of the Volunteer force in Newton. There was a certain amount of heated discussion in the local township because of the rivalry between the Print works owned by George McCorquodale and the Sugar works owned by Joseph Hornby Birley. In the end there were two volunteer corps raised, the 73rd and the 49th, known respectively as 'McCorquodales' and 'Birleys'.

A year later George McCorquodale was present at the formation of the Liverpool Press Guard at a series of meetings held at St George's Hall, Liverpool. George became Lieutenant Colonel of the force. He retained that post for 8 years before retiring from active service. The members of the force then insisted on him taking the honorary title of Colonel, a title he kept and used for the rest of his life. The Liverpool Press Guards eventually became part of the 6th V.B. (King's), Liverpool Regiment early in the 20th century.

After the terrible mining disaster at Wood Pit in 1878 George McCorquodale was made executive Chairman of the Haydock Explosion Relief Fund. Over a number of years he used his organisation skills to raise money for the large number of dependents of those killed. His family also contributed their time and effort by organising bazaars and other events to raise money.

In 1882 George McCorquodale was made High Sheriff of Lancashire, serving for the customary term of 1 year. High Sheriffs are responsible for the courts and judges of the county. The office was a very ancient order but had become largely ceremonial. By the nineteenth century the people who were awarded the honour were industrialists, politicians and landowners. His inaugural banquet was held with great pomp at the Queen's Hotel, Manchester on the 21st April 1882. George was also appointed as Deputy Lieutenant of Lancashire. Lord Lieutenants represent the monarch in the county and are usually members of the peerage. The Deputy Lieutenants were chosen by the county Lord Lieutenant to assist him in his duties. George was appointed and served William Molyneux, Earl of Sefton.

The Banquet Menu to the Grand Jury by George McCorquodale. It was held at the Queen's Hotel, Manchester. The hotel, since demolished, was on the corner of Portland Street and Piccadilly

General Election, 1885.

Mc.Corquodale for Newton Division

COL. Mc.CORQUODALE

Will ADDRESS

His Friends and Supporters, at the

NEW ASSEMBLY HALL, Prescot,

On Tuesday next, Nov. 24.

SPEAKERS :

Professor SHELDON,
(Candidate for Ormskirk Division.)

Lieut.-Col. W. W. PILKINGTON,

Rev. Jas. JOHNSTON,

Mr. Alderman JOHNSON,
(Of St. Helens.)

Captain DUFFY, (of St. Helens),

And other gentlemen.

Doors open at 7 o'clock, Chair to be taken at 7-30, by

W. TYRER, ESQ.

Wood & Co., Printers, Hardshaw Street, St. Helens.

Election campaign poster – 1885

In politics George McCorquodale had always been an enthusiastic Liberal, although it must be said he was of the older, more conservative, school. He attempted to represent his country as an MP twice in his life. In 1880 he and a Mr. J. Lancaster contested the Wigan election as Liberal candidates against Lord Lindsay and Mr. P. Knowles, but they were defeated. In 1885 he tried again and became the Liberal candidate for the Newton Division of Lancashire. His Conservative opponent was Sir Richard Cross and the contest proved to be a highly contested one. George McCorquodale was supported in his campaign by many local dignitaries. Men such as Joseph Evans, the Haydock coal proprietor, Richard and Charles Pilkington of the famous St Helens glass company and William Gamble the son of David Gamble, who was the first Mayor of St Helens and the builder of the Gamble Institute, all supported his claim to be the Newton MP. One problem that George had was that his opponent was an established and proven politician having been Home Secretary recently in his career. The campaign became very intense with claims and counter claims flying back and forth between the rival camps. Polling was very heavy; out of a total register of 9,344 no fewer than 8,506 votes were recorded. Sir Richard Cross was successful with a majority of 383 votes, although George McCorquodale was congratulated on the hard fight he had put up.

Afterwards George penned a letter to all his supporters thanking them for all their efforts:-

"The Willows, Newton-le-Willows

2nd Dec. 1885

After a very hard fight I have been defeated by a small majority. All concerned must feel glad that this election has in the main been contested in a spirit of moderation and good temper leaving no bitterness behind. I now desire to give my sincere thanks to any chairman, Agent, Committee and all who have so willingly given their time and labour in our almost successful vindication of the cause of Liberalism in this division of the County. I feel sure that your splendid efforts on this occasion have not been altogether in vain, but will secure a good prospect of victory for the next Candidate whom you may invite to fight the Liberal battle in your next Contest. With grateful recollections of the considerations that has been shown to me.

I remain

Yours Faithfully

Geo. McCorquodale"

His son-in-law Charles Hamilton was more successful and was returned as MP for Rotherhithe in the same election. It was a district in Southeast London part of the Borough of Southwark, not too far from The Armoury one of the printing houses of the McCorquodale Company. After 1886 and the great split that occurred in the Liberal party George became a supporter of the Liberal Unionist Party, a splinter group of the Liberal Party. The Liberal Unionist Party supported the Conservative Party in the next election enabling them to form a stable government. He had been a Liberal all his life but by then was opposed to the reformist views of the leader of the party, William Gladstone. It was said locally that on one of Gladstone's later visits to the township, George attempted to get his groom to tip William Gladstone out of his carriage by speeding round a corner!

Aerial view of Newton early in the twentieth century.
George McCorquodale's house, The Willows is on the right and on the extreme left is Brookside, the home of Joseph Hornby Birley

Leisure Pursuits

By the 1870s George McCorquodale had become a wealthy man. Hard work, shrewdness and good judgement had produced a thriving printing company. In the 1871 census he proudly gave his profession as 'Magistrate, Landowner, and Printer employing several hundreds of people in the trade of Printer Stationer at London, Glasgow and Newton-le-Willows.' He had seven live-in staff and a number of other staff in the local area. His leisure pursuits were those of the gentry, shooting, fishing and sailing in Scotland. Family sources state that he rented a sporting estate in Kintyre, Scotland and spent many pleasurable holidays there.

George McCorquodale's summer residence Gadlys, Anglesey. A photograph taken in the present day it shows the remnants of a larger building

In the summer months one of George's greatest loves was yachting near to Anglesey in the Menai strait and by the 1880s he normally stayed in a property on the edge of the strait at Craigy don. In 1882 an estate came up for sale just a few miles away and it must have caught his eye. The sale of the Gadlys Estate at the Bull Hotel, Llangefni was on the 26th October 1882. The sale notice from the time showed that George McCorquodale purchased the estate for £14,256 - probably worth in the region of £1 million today. Gadlys was to be his summer residence until his death in 1895. After the purchase he immediately began to extend it and also took a great interest in the local church, St.Sadwrn, Llansadwrn. The attention he gave to Gadlys and The Willows are similar. Both are close to the local church, he extended both buildings and paid out for restructuring of the churches. Gadlys was an ideal place for George McCorquodale. He loved the area, he loved the yachting and the railways brought him to the doorstep. North Wales and Anglesey attracted many of the South Lancashire industrialists. They had new wealth and they used it to buy summer retreats for themselves and their families. An example was his close friend Joseph Evans, the coal owner of Haydock, who lived at Hurst House, Huyton, but had extensive estates in Llanrwst and Llandoggert.

St. Sadwrn's Church, Llansadwrn, Anglesey

A very important photograph of George McCorquodale and his family.
It was taken at The Willows, his house in Newton. Probably taken on his 75th birthday it shows his immediate family, his in-laws and some of his grandchildren. Back row first from the left is Norman McCorquodale, third from the left is Harold McCorquodale, fifth from the left is Rev. Henry Sherlock, seventh from the left is George Frederick McCorquodale and tenth from the left is Alexander Cowan McCorquodale. The young man seated on the floor is Hugh Stewart McCorquodale who was killed at Spion Kop in 1900. The lady in the dark outfit seated immediately behind him is Mary McCorquodale the wife of George Frederick

Churches

Throughout the latter part of his life George McCorquodale was deeply involved in two churches. The first was St. Peter's in Newton and the other was St. Sadwrn, Anglesey. St. Peter's church has been at the end of the main street of Newton for hundreds of years. At various times it has been a chapel of ease for Winwick, a private chapel for the Legh family and the parish church of Newton. St. Peter's church has changed many times over the years and 1891 George McCorquodale was involved in the building of a new chancel. He provided money towards the cost of the construction and on 10th May 1892 he laid the foundation stone in the presence of Dr. Ryle, the Bishop of the diocese. The stone can clearly be seen today with its inscription: - "This stone was laid by George McCorquodale D.L. on the 10 day of May 1892". The building of the new chancel, which was slightly bigger than the old, resulted in the east wall being positioned over the tomb of his first wife. The church was further improved after the death of George McCorquodale when a decision was made by his children to rebuild the nave in the memory of their father. The interior of St. Peter's has a large number of McCorquodale memorials and plaques installed or gifted to the church over the years. The organ was given to the church after the death of Louisa Kate McCorquodale, George's first wife. Paid for totally by her husband at a cost of £600 it still stands there in the modern church today.

St. Peter's Church, Newton after the new Chancel. The foundation stone for the chancel was laid by George McCorquodale on 10th May 1892. Its construction resulted in the back wall of the church being over part of his wife's grave.

St. Peter's Church, Newton after the new nave. Money for the nave was provided by the McCorquodale family after the death of George McCorquodale

The bust of George McCorquodale
St. Peter's Church, Newton

Also in the church there is a memorial to Hugh Stewart McCorquodale, George's youngest son and a marble bust of George McCorquodale. The bust was on display at the colour card section of the Newton works for a number of years but had previously resided at Cardington Street and then moved to the main offices at Basingstoke after the Second World War. It is a classic styled head and shoulders bust in marble showing George in a Roman emperor pose. The bust's arrival in Newton formed part of a very amusing story. In the 1980s, when the company was in its death throes, one of the Newton drivers, Ken Burns, was dispatched with all speed to snatch the said bust from Basingstoke, which he did with great style in the work's van. The bust rested for a while in the colour card department before being donated to St. Peter's Church.

The church of St. Sadwrn in Llansadwrn village on Anglesey is 2 miles west of Beaumaris and about 4 miles from the Menai Bridge. It is situated only a few hundred yards from Gadlys, the Welsh home of George McCorquodale.

Throughout his time at Gadlys George used and supported this small Welsh chapel. The interior is very attractive and contains a number of McCorquodale memorials. There is a dedication to George McCorquodale installed after his death and various examples of the McCorquodale crest on the fitments. Other memorials in the church are two plaques – one to Hugh Stewart McCorquodale and the other to George Lockart Greenshields, George McCorquodale's grandsons both killed in the Boer War. Also there are two lovely stained glass windows dedicated to Hugh Stewart McCorquodale. The graveyard of the church is dominated by a massive Celtic cross, dedicated to Hugh Stewart McCorquodale, supposedly designed by his mother, but erected by the people of Llansadwrn parish.

Photograph of George McCorquodale taken inside The Willows in the 1890s. It shows George relaxing in front of the fire reading his newspaper accompanied by his second wife Emily and his favourite dog

Death

At some time in the early 1890s George McCorquodale suffered a severe seizure, probably a stroke, which caused a complete retirement from business to seek rest and recuperation. For a time he rallied and family and friends lived in the hope that he would recover. But it was not to be and George McCorquodale died at Gadlys on 16th July 1895 surrounded by his family. At Newton the news was received with great sadness and St. Peter's church bell tolled solemnly for most of the day, showing the respect the town had for the man. He was laid to rest in the graveyard of St. Sadwrn Church, Llansadwrn, Anglesey, close by his summer residence. On the morning of the funeral the body was moved from Gadlys to the church by the workmen from the estate, the bearers being the gardeners led by Mr. Hughes the head gardener. Firstly in the church a private service was held for the servants and family. The Rev. E. Evans, rector of Llansadwrn officiated, assisted by the Rev. H. Sherlock, the son-in-law of George McCorquodale. In the afternoon there was a public service at the church conducted by the Revs. E. Evans and R. H. Williams, vicar of Llanfaethu. Present at both services were the choristers of Bangor Cathedral, under the leadership of Mr. Westlake Morgan, cathedral organist. They rendered the funeral hymns – "On the Resurrection Morning," "Now the Labourer's Task is O'er" and "The King of Love My Shepherd Is." The funeral had a large attendance. In addition to the relatives and friends of the deceased, representatives of the commercial undertakings he had founded and large numbers of his tenants were present. All of the sections of his large family were represented at the funeral and the managers from the different printing houses attended.

The final resting place of George McCorquodale in St. Sadwrn's Church graveyard

There were over 60 wreaths sent to the church from individuals and groups such as workers at Newton, servants at the Willows, the 6th V. B. King's (Liverpool Regiment), the Leeds employees, the little children Greenshields and many more. In Newton there was a similar service held for the people who could not travel to Wales. It was also well attended. There was no return to Newton to the place of his great triumphs – he rests in a place he loved. He is the sole occupant of the grave, no second wife, no children. The stone is pink marble very similar to the one where his first wife rests at St. Peter's Church, Newton. From his grave the ground slopes down towards the Menai Strait, an area he loved and enjoyed. In the distance are the mountains of Snowdonia, a stunning view of great beauty.

Legacy

George McCorquodale's will was finally proved by February 1896. The executors were George Frederick McCorquodale, Alexander Cowan McCorquodale, Robert Low Greenshields esquires and Charles Sanderson, solicitor. The final total was £439,396: 10s: 3d, although many of his assets had probably been split between the family beforehand. At his death he left a thriving successful company. The number of printing houses he established served the company for many years to come, some of them surviving until the 1960s. All of the following began in the Victorian age – Liverpool Printing & Stationery; Newton-le-Willows; Cardington Street, London; Caxton Works, Maxwell Street, Glasgow; Wolverton, Buckinghamshire; The Armoury, St. Thomas' Street, London; Leeds, Gutenberg Buildings, Basinghall Street.

George had provided an excellent education for all of his four surviving sons of his first marriage and had taken them into the company. The eldest, George Frederick, had joined the firm in 1871 and shortly after became a partner. He was one of the original directors when the firm became a limited company in 1880. After the death of his father he became chairman, a position he held until his retirement in 1920. Amongst other ventures he was the chief mover in the purchase of Henry Blacklock & Co. of Manchester. The next son, Alexander Cowan, was also one of the original directors of the limited company. He succeeded George Frederick as chairman and was also chairman of the North Wales Paper Company and the Liverpool Printing and Stationery Company, where he paid particular attention to the White Star Shipping Company contract.

The Newton works in the 1920s. It can be seen that the original facade of the Old Conservative Hall was kept and the factory built behind. The Old Legh Arms Hotel has been replaced with a modern office block

The third surviving son, Norman, started his business career at the North Wales Paper Company where he worked for several years. He became a director in the family firm in 1889, and succeeded Alexander Cowan as chairman, a position he held until his death. The last of the sons of George McCorquodale and his first wife was Harold who was also appointed a director in 1889, a position he held for the rest of his life. He started his training at Newton but was soon brought down to head office in London where he served until his death in 1943. Harold never became chairman preferring to pass the position to one of the up and coming younger generation of McCorquodales. He was especially interested in the Post Office and Stationery Office contracts at Wolverton and the Southern Railway contract at the Armoury. The four sons lived like princes, residing in grand houses such as Rossway House and Beechwood Park, Hertfordshire; Cound Hall, Shropshire; Winslow Hall, Buckinghamshire and Forest Hall, Essex. His daughters had married into wealthy, successful and influential families, indicating just how far the family had come from the cottage on the edge of Liverpool.

The military legacy that George McCorquodale left became apparent when the fighting records of the 20th Century are examined. They became a great military family carrying on a tradition began by George with his close association with the Volunteer Forces of Newton and Liverpool. In the twentieth Century the McCorquodales spilled their blood in all of the great conflicts of the 20th century and many of them were awarded medals for their endeavours. Their military connections carried on even up to the present day.

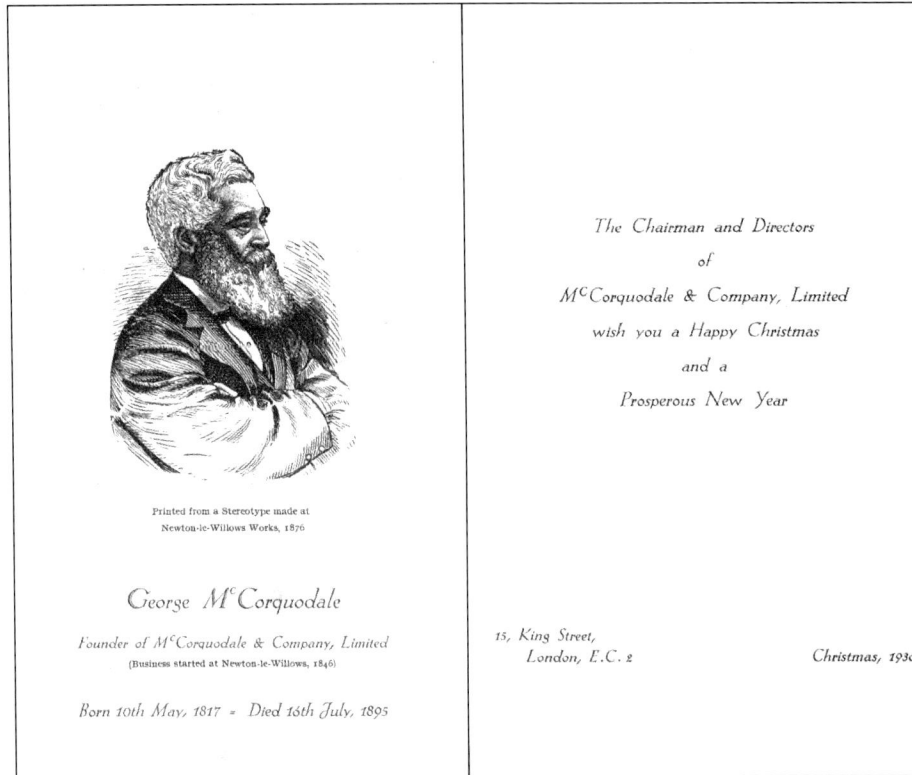

Printed from a Stereotype made at
Newton-le-Willows Works, 1876

George McCorquodale

Founder of McCorquodale & Company, Limited
(Business started at Newton-le-Willows, 1846)

Born 10th May, 1817 - Died 16th July, 1895

The Chairman and Directors
of
McCorquodale & Company, Limited
wish you a Happy Christmas
and a
Prosperous New Year

15, King Street,
London, E.C. 2   Christmas, 1936

Company Christmas and New Year greeting card to employees 1936

Another great legacy that George left was how he dealt with his workforce. He may have been patriarchal and controlling but it worked for the company and satisfied his employees. In the late 1840s and 1860s he readily agreed a number of times to reduce working hours. He was frequently prepared to meet personally with representatives from all departments to inform them of trade aspects and dealings. As far back as 1850 he organised parties and balls for workers and dignitaries in the old Conservative Hall. The building had recently been lighted by gas so it would have been quite a spectacular event in the Newton township.

Regarding workers relations one of his quotes should have gone down in history:-

"the unbound duty of employers is to remember their employed".

His attitude produced a loyal workforce and it was reflected in the long term employment of individual workers. Men and women worked for the company for 25, 30 and even 40 years. Full families carried on a tradition of working for McCorquodales, generation after generation, even after the death of the founder, even up to the demise of the firm. The prime example of loyalty was Herbert Meacham. He began on the shop floor, rose to become manager at the Wolverton works and then became a director of the company. Herbert worked for McCorquodales for 60 years and at his retirement thirteen members of the family were present to wish him well!

However his greatest legacy must be the firm he founded – McCorquodale & Co. It went on to do great things in the printing industry, a company of which the family and the people that worked there in all the many "houses" should be justly proud. Throughout the twentieth century McCorquodales never lost their connection with the railway companies but they also branched out into other printing fields. They designed and developed the colour card system in the 1940s. The process of producing exact colours was a massive boon to the painting industry. It began in the factory at Newton and was copied all across the globe. Also in the twentieth century the company became deeply involved in security printing, producing a large percentage of cheques and bank orders for the banking industry. Throughout the lifetime of the company they produced books in many different fields such as children's books, works on religion, furniture and royal events to name a few. The name of McCorquodale spread all over the world, possessing factories in countries as far afield as Canada, Australia, USA, Brazil, New Zealand, France, Germany, South Africa, Singapore, Nigeria and even in an obscure place such as Khartoum, Sudan. The company produced the majority of the printing memorabilia for the 1948 London Olympics, the 1966 World Cup and many other sporting events.

NEWTON-LE-WILLOWS

From Cardington Street N.W.1

Title pages for the differe
works connected to
George McCorquodale

CAXTON WORKS GLASGOW

LIVERPOOL

WOLVERTON

The McCorquodales themselves rose in British society to the level of the aristocracy. One member of the family was appointed Lady in Waiting to the Duchess of Gloucester. The grandson of George McCorquodale, Malcolm Stewart McCorquodale was ennobled and took the name of Lord McCorquodale of Newton. On the sporting front Alastair McCorquodale, the great grandson of George, became a great athlete and was known as the fastest white man in the 1948 London Olympics. On the literary side, Barbara Cartland, the prolific authoress, married into the family twice. In the present day Colin McCorquodale, the great grandson of George McCorquodale, due to his interest in travel has personally visited every country in the world and every state in the USA.

All the wealth and prestige of the modern day family is a tribute to the hard work, ambition, endeavour and foresight of one man - George McCorquodale - The Master Printer. The name of McCorquodale has all but disappeared from the local communities of Newton, Glasgow, Leeds, London and other places that possessed works and factories. The name may have disappeared but should not be forgotten.

George McCorquodale and the four surviving sons
that carried on his work in the company

Back: George McCorquodale sailing with his family on the Firth of Clyde.
In the background is the island of Ailsa Craig.
It was painted by Ernest Gustave Girardot (1840-1904) in 1871.
He was a British artist known for painting children.
This painting was in the main office of McCorquodale &Co. Ltd.,
King Street, London for many years. It is now in the hands of the family.

Opposite:

Top: London & North Western Railway Timetable – 1909.

Middle: Caledonian Railway Timetable – 1884.

Bottom: Memorial Tablet to George McCorquodale – St. Sadwrn's Church, Anglesey.